Items should be returned on or before the last date shown below. Items
may be renewed by personal application, writing, telephone or by
accessing the online Catalogue Service on Fingal Libraries' website.
To renew give date due, borrower ticket number and PIN number if using
online catalogue. Fines are charged on overdue items and will include
postage incurred in recovery. Damage to, or loss of items will be charged
to the borrower.

Date Due	Date Due	Date Due

SMASHED IN THE USSR

SMASHED IN THE USSR

Fear, Loathing and Vodka on the Steppes

Caroline Walton
&
Ivan Petrov

*with illustrations
by Natalia Vetrova*

OLD STREET PUBLISHING

First published in 2013 by Old Street Publishing Ltd,
Trebinshun House, Brecon LD3 7PX
www.oldstreetpublishing.co.uk

ISBN 978 1 908699 22 0

To Andrei

Contents

... there is nothing either good or bad, but thinking makes it so: to me it is a prison.
Hamlet

Preface

London

2001

The phone rings late on Sunday evening. A man's voice speaks in Russian. He introduces himself as Slava, a friend of Ivan Petrov's.

"I'm with the police at Ivan's flat," the voice falters. "He died this morning. We found your number in his book. The police want to know if you will interpret for us."

Ivan is dead. The words sound strange. Like a lie.

Constable Astwood's careful English voice explains that there will be a post mortem. Automatically, in words that come from somewhere beyond my conscious mind, I relay the information to Slava in Russian.

Slava reassures me that Ivan died in his sleep.

"Was he drinking again?"

Another pause. "He was."

Constable Astwood is back on the line. "There is one more thing…"

"Yes?"

"I notice the deceased had a lot of books. Is there anyone who might take them? If not, the council will only burn them."

I struggle to absorb this kindness. "Yes, yes of course. I'll arrange it. Tomorrow. Thank you."

***

I first met Ivan in 1996. He contacted me after reading a book I had written about life in provincial Russia.[1] He was here as a refugee, he said, seeking political asylum. He wanted to talk to me. I knew where he came from and he liked what I had written.

In the early nineties I had gone to live in the Samara region of Russia where Ivan's home town of Chapaevsk lay. My fascination with the country had been sparked by an introduction to Dostoevsky in my teens; with the fall of the USSR I was free to explore it. Samara's military installations had closed the area to westerners since the end of the Second World War. Many parts of the region were also off-limits to locals, apart from those with special permits. I wanted to know what life had been like behind that inner iron curtain. I arrived in 1992, just after the collapse of Soviet power. Compared to Moscow and other more accessible regions, the area was slow to change.

Chapaevsk was an industrial satellite of the city of Samara. I made several trips there to visit friends, and each time I returned with my head throbbing from the polluted air. Founded in 1911 and built up around a gunpowder factory, the town began as Ivashchenko, became Trotsk from 1919 until Trotsky's exile in 1929; and ended up as Chapaevsk in honour of the Civil War hero. It was, in my friends' words, "a town of death" – a contaminated pit of chemical and pesticide plants, ringed by secret military installations.

"Everyone was horrified when Chernobyl blew up," they said, "but we have absorbed this poisoned atmosphere all our lives."

Their daughter was in hospital with a blood disorder. We would stand in the hospital grounds while she lowered a

---

1   *Little Tenement on the Volga* (Garrett County Press).

basket on a rope to receive books and foodstuffs. She was not allowed visitors for fear of infection. Later I was taken to the local orphanage, where many of the children suffered from skin diseases and serious developmental problems.

In the 1920s Chapaevsk began manufacturing chemical weapons for Germany, which was banned from making its own under the Treaty of Versailles. During World War Two, phosgene, mustard gas and Lewisite were produced for the USSR's own use. After the war the plants were converted to the production of the now-banned pesticide lindane and its derivatives, liquid chlorine and other chlorinated chemicals. Emissions from these plants contained highly toxic dioxins. Slow to degrade, they lingered in the environment and accumulated in the food chain. In 1994 a United Nations special commission called the town an ecological disaster zone.

I was touched by the spirit of the people who lived in this forlorn, devastated region of smokestacks and phosphorescent green lakes.

"You've seen a lot," Ivan said, when we first met at the Britain-Russia Centre on Grosvenor Place, "but I will tell you much more."

A short, bearded man, he walked with the aid of a stick. His right leg scythed backwards, giving his whole body an impression of concavity. He had the squashed nose of a prize fighter, sparse teeth, and intelligent blue eyes. A crude sailing ship was tattooed on his forearm just above his wrist. In his early sixties, he looked ten years older.

"You want to know what it was like growing up there?" he grinned. "Well I'll tell you! Do you mind if I smoke?"

We walked outside onto Grosvenor Place. Propping himself

against the railings, Ivan hooked his stick over his arm and rolled a cigarette. I strained to catch his Russian above the roar of traffic. "You see," he cupped the flame of a match against the wind, "I was born in 1934. During the years when I grew up, it made no difference which side of the barbed wire you lived on." He leaned back and exhaled. "Prisoners in camps, collective farmers, factory workers – it was all the same."

Across the road barbed wire clouded the walls around Buckingham Palace gardens.

"You had a choice," he continued, "you could carve out a career for yourself as an informer or bureaucrat; or else seek a way out."

"And what did you do?"

"I was a sailor, a meteorologist in the Siberian taiga, a labourer in the Tien Shan mountains, but first and foremost I was a drunk." He beamed. "Not an ordinary, drink-up-your-wage-packet drunk, or even a flog-your-house-and-furniture drunk, but a vagabond and a beggar."

I was intrigued. "I thought it was forbidden to be a tramp in the Soviet Union?"

"It was. If they caught you they banged you up. I did a few years in camps. Still, I spent long enough on the road." He pulled an empty matchbox from his pocket and tucked his extinguished cigarette end into it: "I am Ivan the Fifth!"

"Pleased to meet you. Why the Fifth?"

"You've heard of Ivan the Terrible?"

"Certainly."

"Well he was the 'Fourth,' so I am the Fifth. Ivan the Drunk! But I am not drinking now and I want to tell you my story."

I had already written about the lives of people of his region:

collective farmers, a wise woman who told fortunes, the new businessmen... But this man was offering to take the lid off the 'lower depths' of Soviet society, a world virtually unknown in the west. I had read a lot of gulag literature, most of it written by men and women from a different class of society, from the intelligentsia, or somewhere fairly close to those circles. Beside me was someone of an altogether different order.

But it went deeper than intellectual curiosity. As I stood listening to Ivan I recalled another man – also named Ivan – whom I had known in Samara. A young businessman who had been brought up in a children's home, he had a similar enthusiasm for talking about subjects most people preferred to hide, a cheerfulness, an ability to 'laugh through tears,' as the Russians say. I missed that quality.

I missed the country too. Standing beside Ivan on a dusty London street, I no longer saw the red buses and black taxis. I was back on the bridge of a Volga pleasure cruiser, steering it downriver, the city on the left bank, blue steppe-land rolling away on the other. Behind me the great river wound its way back towards the gelid lakes and marshes of the north; before me it coursed for a thousand kilometres down to the Caspian Sea. Excited to have a foreigner aboard, the captain had let me take the helm. The expansiveness and exhilaration of that voyage epitomised what I loved about Russia. Life was harsher than at home but at the same time less constrained. Back then, in the early nineties, it had seemed as though anything were possible.

"What about money?" I hauled myself back to the present: "And there's no guarantee that the book will find a publisher..." I was guessing that this man shared the usual unrealistic Russian hopes of the West.

Ivan waved his hand in dismissal. "I don't need money; I want my story to be told."

Like a latter-day Ancient Mariner. We never mentioned the subject of money again.

I arrived for our first session at Ivan's address in Hackney. He lived in a substantial Victorian terrace carved up into a warren of units that sheltered the newly-arrived. I hesitated by the bell. Above it 'Ivan the Fifth' was scrawled in Cyrillic letters on the rough paintwork of the wall. How much of his life would this man be able to remember? He had not had a drink for a year, he told me. He had been writing down his memories.

The slow thump of Ivan's stick approached the door. He ushered me into a communal hall where giggling Somali children tumbled over a musty carpet. We went upstairs to the two-roomed flat he shared with another asylum-seeker. An entire wall was lined with books: politics, history and classics, in Russian and English. He could read English with the help of a dictionary, he said, although he spoke it badly.

He had prepared a meal of *adzhap sandal* – Georgian vegetable stew. Then we watched a Soviet film: *The Cold Summer of '53*, about a struggle between criminal and political prisoners. That was to become our pattern. Each week or fortnight we would spend an afternoon together, Ivan smoking and drinking strong black tea while I ate the excellent lunches he prepared. Afterwards we would discuss the work-in-progress and then watch an old film. Some, like *Cold Summer*, were about a facet of life that Ivan wanted me to understand; occasionally we would enjoy a Soviet romantic comedy that evoked a lost, more innocent age. As I left Ivan would hand me a tape with a recording of the next instalment of his story. Later, he bought a second hand typewriter and gave me a few pages each week, which saved me the chore of transcribing words that were not always clear, consonants often vanishing through gaps where his teeth had fallen out.

As we worked, I crosschecked factual details. Later I had an English-speaking Russian check a draft of the story for authenticity, for nuances that I as a foreigner might have missed. My reader said he laughed his way through much of the tale: "That was our lives!"

Ivan's long-term memory seemed remarkably intact. Although his drinking bouts had generally ended in blackout, he was able to describe the periods between drinking sessions, including his years in prison camps where he – usually – could not get hold of alcohol. There had also been times when alcohol failed to bring the oblivion he craved. Then he recalled his physical and mental agony in searing detail. In fact, it may have been the 'dry' periods – sometimes extending for a couple of years or more, that saved Ivan from developing alcoholic dementia, like those sufferers he saw in his many sobering-up hospitals.

A discrepancy emerged between the character he portrayed and the way I saw him. He was always solicitous of my well-being. When my computer broke down he arranged for a friend of his to sell me one cheaply and help me install it. When I was recovering from flu he brought me honey sent over from his nephew's beehives near Chapaevsk. On the occasions when we worked in my flat he never arrived empty-handed. He brought ingredients and taught me to cook Russian dishes.

One day in December I pressed my front door buzzer to admit Ivan. He seemed to take longer than usual on the stairs. The thumps of his stick slowed. I opened the door to see Ivan climbing the last few stairs, bent over beneath a Christmas tree he was hauling on his back: "For you, Caroline." He always addressed me by the respectful '*vui*' form of the Russian 'you.'

The warmth and generosity of the real life Ivan were missing from his story, but I understood that years of drinking had eroded his self-esteem to the bone. He wanted to relieve himself of his memories as honestly as he could and I trusted him all the more because he painted himself in such a bleak light.

As I listened to Ivan an understanding grew – a sense of familiarity. At first I put this down to environment. I had seen the factories Ivan described and the football stadium where he watched his local team – except by 1993 the stands had collapsed.

But it was more than that; I recognised the features of Ivan's internal landscape: his self-destructive behaviour and his justifications for it. Over the course of two years he recounted his life with a logic I never had to question. For I was essentially no different to him; I reacted to alcohol as he did. If I had one glass I needed a dozen more, just as some people have to finish the whole box of chocolates.

There was a time when alcohol gave me a sense of elation and invulnerability – like being at the helm of that Volga cruiser with a Kalashnikov by my side. Inevitably, the effect began to diminish and it took longer to recover from drinking sessions. Work was an irritation; friends were confined to those who could match my capacity. I shared Ivan's restlessness. He tramped the Soviet Union; I travelled the globe. When things didn't go my way I blamed others, just as Ivan did. But I could not believe I was an alcoholic, for they were people like him who lived on garbage dumps. And I never drank anti-dandruff lotion, although I did develop a taste for *samogon* – Russian home-distilled spirits.

When I first arrived in Samara people would take me into their bathrooms and show me their stills. I congratulated myself on my choice of destination. Then one night I walked home after a dinner party, oblivious to the cold, entranced by starlight on snow. I ended up in hospital. The Kazakh urologist told me to stay off the vodka and for a while I heeded his advice.

As I pieced together Ivan's story I recognised the rationales, the fear, the self-obsession and the compulsion. He described it all so vividly that I felt as though I were looking into a mirror.

We never drank together; neither of us wanted to drink. In our own ways we used the book as a life buoy, letting go at the end and swimming off in opposite directions.

At times it hurt Ivan to relive episodes of his life – particularly those that involved his wife and daughter. Looking back, I probably should not have been surprised when he went silent for a month. No one answered the phone. I started to worry, fearing the worst. I dreaded to think that the work we had begun might have been in vain. Finally a call came. A hoarse voice invited me round.

"Yes, I drank." Ivan admitted. "I had the dt's. I went to hospital. They refused to give me anything to help. They probably thought I was a drug addict too."

Tea spilled from the cup he handed to me.

"I'm sorry," he apologised, "I haven't written anything this time. But I will. I'm better now."

His eyes were unfocused, as though no one was home.

The following week we carried on as usual.

But then, as we neared the end of his story, I had a call.

"Caroline, help me. I am going to die tonight."

I went through the local directory, trying all the treatment centres listed. Eventually a place in the Elephant and Castle agreed to admit him. But a few days later they phoned. They had had to ask Ivan to leave. He had smuggled in vodka in a hot water bottle. I called him at home. He was barely coherent. I slammed down the phone in futile rage.

I was afraid the book would not be finished.

But at Christmas he called to wish me well. We made it up. I went to visit him at his new flat. A Georgian restaurant was paying him to make homemade meat dumplings. His ex-wife had been in touch he said. He sounded happy. We resumed the work.

And then, finally, Slava's call came.

***

Ivan left a haunting legacy: the lower depths of the Soviet Union refracted through his alcoholic mind. Some of the people he talks about in his book are still alive; I have changed his name and theirs in order to protect their identity. I have kept Ivan's voice in the first person – the way he narrated his story to me.

1

A Town of Death

The 1940s

Sirens wail as gas clouds billow through the market-place. Pressing scarves to our noses we run with other shoppers towards the gate. Stall-holders flee too, deserting bunches of herbs, beetroot and meat-bones. "It's plant Number 14 again," yells a woman behind us.

Our block of flats is swathed in yellow fog. We run upstairs, secure the windows and sit down to wait for the radio dish in the kitchen to give the all-clear. I feel safe behind concrete and glass but I worry about the families who live in the wooden workers' barrack huts below us.

"Ma, what about the people in the barracks? Maybe the gas will get through their walls and poison them?"

"They'll be all right."

As the wind changes the fog begins to thin. Stalin emerges through the mist, rooted to his platform in front of our factory's board of honour. One by one the chimneys of our chemical plants reappear. At last I can see our Chapaevsk pyramids – the great piles of Caspian sea salt that Volga barges dump beside our chlorine plant.

The district where we live is called Bersol, after our local factory, which manufactures potassium chlorate. Its managers and chief engineers live in our block of flats; shop-floor workers are housed in the barracks.

Half a mile down the road there is a TNT plant where prisoners work. In the morning I watch them leave their camp by the railway embankment. When dusk falls and the searchlights come on they shuffle home again with bowed heads. Dogs snap at their heels. I wonder if my father is among those grey figures.

***

"You know Ivan's father was a Chekist,[2] my grandmother whispers to a neighbour. I don't understand her, although I know that the man who lives with us is not my real father. I dimly remember another man, a tall figure walking through the front door with a metal basin on his head. I haven't seen that man for a long time.

"Ma, where's that other man who used to live here?"

My mother is standing in the kitchen, slicing onions with her back to me. She pauses: "He's in prison. Forget about him."

"Can I send him my drawing of the *Cutty Sark*?"

My mother lays down her knife on the chopping board. "He's not allowed to receive letters," she snaps without turning round.

***

My stepfather's belt is studded like a Cossack's. At school they ask questions about the marks on my skin. I don't know what to say. I'm afraid that if I tell the truth he'll beat me again. The local Party committee summons my parents for a consultation. After that my step-father doesn't beat me so often but instead he keeps me indoors for days at a time.

---

2 The Cheka were the Soviet political police formed by Lenin shortly after the October revolution in 1917.

I sit in our bay window watching my friends kick a clod of frozen horse-dung around the yard. They swoop after their ball like a flock of demented birds. Vovka Bolotin, who is crippled by polio, keeps goal with his crutch. We all envy Vovka, who wields his crutch so deftly it is almost impossible to get the ball past him.

Nelka Ehrlich, who lives in the flat opposite ours, comes to play with my sister and me. The kitchen radio dish broadcasts my favourite song: *Sailing the Seven Seas*. Nelka distracts me, prancing around making faces. I hit her and grab her pigtails. My mother bursts in and pulls us apart. She slaps me but not Nelka.

I run into the toilet, climb onto the seat, loop the washing line round my neck, tie it to a hook and jump. Black circles close in before my eyes.

I lie on the floor looking up at my mother. Her screams hurt my ears. And my neck hurts too. But Nelka and I make it up.

***

We are playing a game in Nelka's flat when suddenly the room starts to shake and dissolve around us. Light bulbs swing, glass shatters and the sideboard topples over onto Nelka's baby brother. The earth roars and shakes. I think I'd better go home. As I cross the landing the floor heaves again. My mother appears in the doorway with my sister in her arms. "Follow me, Vanya!" We run across the street to the factory offices, where a throng of people are hurrying down to the basement shelter.

The door is thick like a submarine's and has a round handle. We sit down to wait. At first we think it's an air raid but we hear no planes. German bombers have never come this far into Russia. Then we guess that one of the munitions factories has blown up. We wait in silence, praying that no spark or ball of flame will drop on Bersol and wipe us all out.

Nelka sits opposite me. She starts to make funny faces again. I stick out my tongue at her, but her eyes begin to bulge until they seem about to burst from their sockets. She coughs and bends her head low. A stream of vomit splashes onto the floor. As she straightens up I see a thin white worm dangling from her lips. Her chest and throat convulse and she spews the worm onto the floor. I watch it lying in the pool of sick and try to imagine it curled up inside Nelka's guts. I want to ask her if the worm tickled but I guess it isn't the right moment.

When the all-clear sounds we climb up to the street. It's covered in glass and rubble and there's a huge piece of concrete stairwell across the entrance to our block. The windows of our flat are gaping black holes spiked with daggers of glass. We set off for my grandmother's house on the edge of town. There is a hard frost. Behind us the red sky crackles with sparks and flames. Sounds of the town fade until the stillness is broken only by my mother's heels clip-clopping on the cobbles.

The next day I pass the hospital. Corpses are piled in the snow, naked and charred like the roasted pig I saw last summer at a country wedding. The TNT plant blew up just as the workers were changing shifts. Dozens were killed, maybe hundreds; no one ever knows the true number. I'm happy because our school is closed for two weeks. Its windows have been blown out.

People say it was sabotage and that our town simpleton, Bathhouse Losha, is a German spy. Bathhouse Losha has never harmed anyone, but a few weeks later he disappears and we never see him again.

***

Chapaevsk lies on a railway line between the Front and the arms factories in the Ural mountains. Trains loaded with broken tanks and weapons stop at our station. Some of us boys distract the guards while the others swarm over the equipment. I undo copper rings from shells and mainsprings from grenades. I know a neighbour who'll give me a couple of roubles for these. We open the hatches of tanks and drop down inside, examining dials and levers, taking them apart to try to understand how they work. When the train jerks and begins to move we scramble out and leap off, rolling down the embankment on the far side of the station.

The prisoners in the camp by the railway line have been sent to the Front. Uzbek and Kirghiz peasants take their place. At first they too were sent off to fight but they didn't understand enough Russian to obey orders. When one was killed his comrades would gather around the corpse and wail. Then they too were cut down by bullets. So instead they join the labour army: changing their kaftans and skull caps for rubber suits and breathing apparatus, they work on production lines filling shells with mustard gas and Lewisite.

My mother is a medical assistant at a munitions plant. She tells me that the Uzbeks are homesick for their mountain pastures and sometimes slip off their gas masks for a minute or two. They hope to fall sick enough to be sent home, or at least to earn a couple of weeks' rest in bed. There are many Uzbek graves in our cemetery.

***

Everyone clutches the person in front of them in case hooligans try to break through the bread queue. A man hurries out of the shop, clutching a loaf to his chest. A small boy hurls himself at the man. He sinks his teeth into the man's wrist, making him yell and drop the loaf. The child falls to his knees and devours the bread right there on the ground. The man kicks him and tries to pull him up but the boy takes no notice. People in the queue tut and grumble but no one moves.

"Well, God sees everything and the poor things are hungry too," says the old lady behind me. There are many homeless kids in our town. They have run away from the Front and the areas under Nazi occupation.

The next morning I watch the boy-thief crawl out from under Stalin's feet. I grab a piece of bread from our kitchen and run downstairs. Feeling a bit scared, I hold out the bread. The boy takes it and stuffs it into his shirt. His face is white and he looks straight through me as blind men do. Before he can run off I say: "My name is Vanya, what's yours?"

"Slavka."

"Why d'you live under the board of honour?" The board is shaped like the Kremlin walls and carries photos of star workers.

"I ran away from a children's home in Kharkov. We starved there. My father was killed on the Front. My mother died when our house was bombed. I'm okay here."

"I can get some potatoes from our store. Come with me and we'll roast them on the slag heap by the TNT plant."

"All right."

I skip school to hang around with Slavka. I admire him almost as much as my literary hero, Robinson Crusoe. His senses are much sharper than mine. If he hears a paper rustle 50 metres away he stiffens like a hunting dog.

I take him to our Zambezi river – the effluent stream running past our plant. It is so hot that it steams even when there is snow all around and we have 20 degrees of frost. Using a board as a raft, we race downstream.

"Vanya," Slavka suggests, "let's run away to the Front. Maybe a regiment will adopt us as sons."

Taking a small bundle of clothes and a loaf under my arm, I creep out of the house to meet Slavka. He shows me how to sneak onto trains. Twice we try to cross the Syzran bridge over the Volga, but soldiers discover us and turn us back. The third time, we manage to wriggle into a dog box fixed underneath a carriage. Although it's summer, the wind is cold. I wrap my jacket tightly around me and close my eyes, picturing the whole map of Russia spread out before us with our locomotive crawling along it like a toy. I want to burst with happiness.

After a long time we emerge at a station. We tell the soldiers there that we're orphans making our way back to liberated territory. Young and kind lads, they give us food and send us on our way. We jump trains, travelling inside now, telling the same story until we reach Kharkov. The city has just been liberated and lies in ruins. It smells worse than the waste-pit behind Chapaevsk's meat-processing plant. Before we can explore we are picked up by female officers, and sent to a children's home in Tambov.

The law of the jungle reigns in that home. Big boys snatch food from the girls and the younger kids. Slavka sticks up for me, but I can't stand the hunger so I confess that I'm not really an orphan. They send me back to Chapaevsk. My stepfather beats me so badly I spend several days in bed. But my mother feeds me. I feel bad about leaving Slavka.

After the war is over a post office form arrives, saying a parcel is waiting for me. My mother takes me to the post office and I hand in my form. It is the first parcel I have ever received. At home I untie the heavy package. Inside is a book from Slavka, a *Herbarium* full of pictures of strange southern plants and flowers. He writes that he is in an orphanage in Moscow. He has won a trip to *Artek*, an elite children's camp in the Crimea. Even Party members' children have to be top students to go there. Slavka writes that he will never forget me, but that is the last I will ever hear from him.

***

We carry our books to school in gas-mask containers lined with plywood. After class we wait by the school gate for the girls. As they come out we hit them with our bags. We're punishing those who tell tales; the rest we hit as a warning.

Worse than the girls are the Young Pioneer leaders who hang back after class to report wrongdoers to the teacher. We despise them and exclude them from our games. In an act of bravado, my friend Tolik throws his red scarf into the classroom stove. A meeting is called. One after another, Pioneer leaders spring to their feet and denounce Tolik with spite in their voices. Afterwards I try to cheer him up: "Never mind Tolik, better be damned than an honest Pioneer!" But he becomes less bold after that.

The Palace of Pioneers is in the former church of Sergei Radonezhsky. The church was once the most beautiful building in Chapaevsk, with mosaic images of saints adorning its facade. It closed after the revolution. During the war it was turned into an armaments store and camouflaged in thick grey plaster. Now the plaster is beginning to fall off. First it crumbles away from the mosaics. A nose emerges, then a forehead, then the stern eye of a saint. As news of the miracle spreads, the town fills with believers. News spreads through forest and steppe, summoning the faithful from as far away as the Ural mountains. The police drive them back but they regroup at a distance from the church.

Our maths teacher, Sava Stepanovich Liga, takes us down to the church after school. He lost a leg in the war and hobbles on crutches. We gather in front of the church while Sava Stepanovich speaks: "It is a very simple phenomenon, explained by the laws of physics. The brickwork is rough so plaster clings to it; mosaics are smooth and plaster falls off them quite easily."

He speaks loudly enough for the faithful to hear, but the old ladies raise their voices so their prayers drown out the words of the heretic. They want to believe their miracle.

Soon afterwards the mosaics are chipped away and a huge glass window is put in their place. On Saturdays we children are sent to help with the work.

After we have helped to build the Palace of Pioneers they send us out to the steppe to plant forests. These bands of trees will stretch from Chapaevsk to the Caspian Sea, and will protect the crops from dry southern winds. In the town we plant saplings around our school and along the streets. At first we care for them, but then the State diverts our energies into a new campaign to collect scrap metal, and the neglected trees wither and die.

***

"*Pale youth with feverish gaze*,"[3] the teacher recites. "This is an example of reactionary poetry. How could a young boy possibly look like that?"

"It's possible," I pipe up.

She peers at me over her glasses. "How?"

"Perhaps he had TB."

---

3 From *To the Young Poet*, by Valerii Bryusov (1873-1924).

The class giggles.

"Out!" roars the teacher. I run past her and soon I'm walking in the spring sunshine, happy to think of the others bending over their books.

I run down to the railway line, climb the embankment and march along the tracks, keeping my eyes fixed on them in the hope of finding a spot where an American spy has undone the bolts. I'll become a hero by running towards an oncoming train waving a red scarf on a stick. But I have nothing red. I wish I hadn't left my Pioneer scarf at school. A character in a book would cut his arm with a piece of glass and soak a handkerchief with his blood. It's a pity handkerchiefs are bourgeois-intellectual relics and I blow my nose with my fingers.

A long-distance train charges past, as though it cares nothing for our town and our lives. The faces flashing by must belong to the happiest people in the world. In the wake of the train I search for empty books of matches. Their town of origin is stamped on rough cardboard: *Vladivostock, Tomsk, Khabarovsk.* The names make my head swim.

At dusk I make my way over to the workers' barracks. Throwing open the outer doors I yell: "Hurrah!" and charge down the corridor, punching the long-johns and bras that dangle overhead. Outside the door of my friend Victor's room I whistle our pirate signal.

"Who's there, friend or foe?"

"Crusoe."

Victor's parents sit at the table eating rye bread and potatoes. His grandparents snore in their bed above the stove and his baby brother bawls unheeded in the corner. Victor and I wrestle on the floor until his parents scream at us to stop. Then Victor picks up his accordion and we sing old folk songs and sea shanties. Even the grandfather gets up from the stove to join in the chorus. I'm so out of tune he laughs: "Eh, Vanya, a bear must've farted in your ears."

Victor and the other boys who live in the barracks used to make fun of me because my parents are Party members and we have a home-help. But they're not malicious and soon grow tired of teasing me. I feel comfortable with them for they aren't ashamed of poverty and have no pretensions.

Some of the barracks' families are so poor the children have only one pair of shoes between them. In bad weather they take it in turns to go to school. I don't want to stand out from the rest so when I leave our flat in the morning I run down to the basement, take off my shoes and hide them behind the hot-water pipes. But I come home from school to find my shoes have gone; my trick has been discovered. My step-father Dobrinin rages while my mother asks why I did it.

"To be like the rest."

"Vanya, there is nothing admirable about poverty. There is no shame in working hard for a better life."

But it is my mother I am ashamed of. She struts through the town like a film star in high heels and expensive dresses. Local children jeer as she passes by with her nose in the air: "There's shit on your shoes, Madame!" They parade in her wake, holding their noses and wiggling their bottoms until they collapse into the mud, hooting with laughter and whistling at her disappearing back. My mother pretends not to hear. She despises the barrack dwellers as only someone who comes from that background can.

***

My step-grandparents live in a dacha at Studioni Avrag, a settlement further up the Volga. Before the revolution the

Dobrinins were members of the nobility. Now they're 'former people' and receive no pension. They survive by growing flowers. Their neighbours say that flowers are useless and that they should grow tomatoes and cucumbers instead. But Granny loves her gladioli and asters. Her fingers are bent and clawed and in the evenings she complains of back ache. After supper she puts on her night-cap and gown and retires with her French novel. She keeps a porcelain chamber-pot under her bed, for nothing will make her visit the earth closet at night.

Grandad is a quiet man but when he speaks it's to the point. He's always busy in his garden. I help look after his two goats, making sure they don't jump over the wall to nibble the neighbours' apple trees. Sometimes they escape and then we hear the neighbour woman chasing them, shouting: "Hey, you Americans, hooligans, get out of here!"

My grandparents have a daughter, Ira. Although she's my stepfather's sister Ira isn't like him at all. Tall, strong and fearless, she rows Granny and me across the Volga for a picnic one day. My mother swims after the boat. She is a good swimmer, but to tease me Granny asks: "Aren't you afraid your mother will drown?"

"No," I reply. "I have Auntie Ira."

My grandparents complain that the new dam being built across the Volga will harm our natural environment, that animals will be driven away and fish will disappear from the river. I know they're wrong. The dam will give electricity to everyone and bring us closer to communism.

Studioni Avrag is a summer resort for professors and doctors. I play with their children. Each year, as August draws to a close, we bid each other farewell until the next summer. But one year, just after the end of the war, few of my playmates return. In their place young and beautiful newcomers arrive in shining black *Emka* limousines. They wear well-cut uniforms and laugh loudly. Through the fence I glimpse lithe figures leaping to catch volley balls. The adults speak about the newcomers in whispers.

I am a white raven amongst these people, for I come from godforsaken Chapaevsk and I tend goats. I have to prove myself. I'm no good at football but I can dive off the river ferries. When the boats tie up at the dock I climb their sides to the third deck and launch myself into the air like a swallow. Last year a boy dived under the ferry's paddle and was killed. Now the sailors keep a strict watch, so it's even more exciting to sneak past them. Finally they catch me and slap tar all over my body. It takes days to clean the tar off, and I get into big trouble at home.

***

An old man is fishing from the quay. He calls me over and points across the Volga. "You see some strange fish in these parts, my lad. Over there is a place called Gavrilova Field. That is where prisoners go to die, full of dysentery and pellagra. They send them from camps all over the country. They're already goners by the time they reach Gavrilova Field."

I run away from the man. For a long time after that I try not to think about the place across the river.

***

I hide behind the latrine with a rock in my hand. Auntie Praskovya waddles through the mud clutching her squares of newsprint. She's a bad-tempered old lady who chases us boys out of her yard because she says we stop her chickens laying. Wood creaks. A sigh. Burying my nose in my collar I lift the trapdoor and hurl my brick into the cess-pit. It splashes. There's a loud

shriek. I run off, glancing back to see Auntie Praskovya pulling up her drawers. "Ivan Petrov, you'll be an alcoholic when you grow up!"

I laugh at her prediction. I don't like alcohol, although I know it's the joy of adult life. I've seen them get drunk often enough. Most people drink meths or some other vodka substitute because the real thing is expensive and hard to get hold of. Besides, you can never tell what has been added to it; everyone knows someone who's died from adulterated vodka.

We call methylated spirits *Blue Danube*. It's sold for lighting primus stoves and is in great demand. It is even drunk at weddings, with fruit syrup added to the women's glasses. My mother usually drinks surgical spirit which she steals from her factory, adding burned sugar to improve the flavour. She sneers at the 'arse-washing' water of the barracks' families, which is home-brew made from hot water, sugar and yeast. Every room has a tub of this muddy liquid bubbling away under a blanket in the corner.

On birthdays and holidays the adults give us children glasses of beer. Knowing what's expected of us we stagger about, clutching at walls. They laugh, but I know the adults also exaggerate their drunkenness. Victor's father once spent a night in the police cells for pissing against a statue of Lenin. "Lucky I was drunk," he said afterwards. "If I'd been sober I'd have got ten years."

***

"Get washed, Vanya," my mother orders. "We have company today."

"But I want to go to Victor's." I hate it when my parents drink.

"Enough! You will stay here."

The visitors arrive.

"Oh Anna Konstantinova, what a marvellous spread!" cries our lady guest.

Ma smirks: "*Quantum satis!*" She has laid out a meal on her best crockery, which Dobrinin brought back from Germany after the war, along with three guns, a cutthroat razor and a radio. He was not an important man and carried away only two suitcases of war trophies, but that's not the impression he gives. According to him, he rode into Berlin on a tank, and he hints that he had the ear of Marshal Konev himself.

At table, Dobrinin dominates the conversation, beginning with his wartime feats before moving on to even more unlikely subjects: "Anton, Anton Pavlovich that is, always said he preferred vodka to philosophy as a hangover cure."

'Chekhov died the year before you were born,' I think to myself, 'not that our guests will say anything. It won't even occur to them that you might not have known him personally. They're too impressed by your aristocratic origins. They wouldn't dream of questioning you.'

Our guests present Dobrinin with a bottle of vodka for the toasts. My stepfather goes to the dresser and rummages around, finally laying his hands on the neck of a cut-glass decanter pillaged from some Prussian farmhouse. As he pulls out the vessel there is a gasp and a giggle. I bolt for of the door.

An egg lies in the bottom of the decanter, the result of one of my experiments. I had heard that eggs lost their shape when soaked in strong vinegar. I tried it and it worked. I rolled the softened egg into a sausage and dropped it into the decanter. Then I poured in cold water and the egg returned to its normal shape, but of course I couldn't retrieve it. I pushed the decanter to the back of the dresser and forgot about it.

I stay out until very late. When I come in Dobrinin is snoring on the sofa and my mother is in bed. In the morning my stepfather begins to recall the outrage of the day before. I run out of the door before he can hit me.

I go to my grandmother's. Granny Nezhdanova lives with her son Volodya in a wooden house built on a pile of slag beside the sulphur plant. Long ago Granny and her husband fetched soil from the steppe to spread around the house but gradually the groundwater rose and poisoned all their plants. Only goosefoot grows as tall as my head. The water from their well is yellow and tastes of TNT. Granny and Volodya live on potatoes, salted cabbage, bread and milk baked in the oven. My mother is ashamed of her family and rarely visits or sends them money. Granny's husband died when I was a baby. She survives by buying needles and thread from a local policeman and selling them in the market.

Uncle Volodya is home and to cheer me up he suggests I come into the city with him. My uncle is only six years older than me. He started work when he was fifteen, but he studies at night school and won a Stalin scholarship to Kuibyshev polytechnic. Volodya is very cheerful and sharp-witted. I'm proud to go out with my tall uncle, even though he always wears felt boots, winter and summer, to work and to dances.

We trot off to the station, swinging a pail of baked milk between us. The local train lurches in and we board without tickets. The carriage is packed with passengers squeezed onto wooden benches, all smoking rough tobacco or nibbling sunflower seeds. The floor crunches as we walk. At a stop further down the line we jump off and run to a carriage that the conductors have already checked.

At each station beggars scramble aboard and shuffle through the carriages, telling stories or singing rhymes. Most are war invalids, missing arms or legs; some have been blinded or burnt in tanks. "I returned half-dead from the Front to find a lieutenant's cap on my peg," says a shabby beggar, holding out his hand. A legless man rolls through on a trolley, rattling a tin.

> *I saw it all, I took Berlin,*
> *I wiped out thirty Hun,*
> *I filled buckets with blood,*
> *So give me something for a drink!*

The beggars have escaped from invalid homes where they rotted with hunger and boredom. They sleep in stations and cold entranceways, with nothing to do but drink to forget their grief. The most unfortunate are the 'samovars,' who lost both their arms and legs. You see them gathered outside markets and stations, begging from their little trolleys. They appeal to their 'dear brothers and sisters,' echoing the words of Stalin during the German advance.

As the train pulls into a suburb of Kuibyshev hideous screams and curses come from the platform. A group of homeless women are fighting their way aboard. They stink of drink and sweat; their bloated faces are bruised. They thrust scrawny babies at passengers as they beg. One of them grabs my arm. "Little son, for the love of God give me something for the baby!"

There's a blackish crust of dried blood where her nose should be. I turn away, curling up on the seat and hugging my knees. I wish I had something to give her.

I enjoy walking around the city with my uncle, meeting up

with his friends and laughing at their jokes. At the end of the day we return to Chapaevsk with our empty pail. As we walk down the muddy lane that leads to her house Granny's voice reaches us: "That puffed-up little tart! Her own mother not good enough for her! Well Nyurochka, what does your fancy man get up to when you're on night shift? Don't come crying to your old mother then!"

Granny is in the throes of her weekly drinking spree. Her padded jacket is torn and her headscarf has fallen off into the mud.

Two policemen are stumbling around in the mud trying to catch her. Nimbly, she dodges their grasp, spins around and launches herself at the nearest man: "Fuck you! Parasite!"

She pushes the policeman so hard that he staggers backwards and sinks up to his knees in a rut. Granny laughs and lies down in the deepest puddle. "Come and get me you old goats!"

Guessing that they won't want to soil their uniforms, she relaxes, shuts her eyes and breaks into a dirty song. Volodya goes up to her. I hang back behind him.

"Come on, Ma, let's go home."

Granny allows him to pull her up and she meekly follows him to the house. Once indoors Volodya takes off her muddy clothes and makes up her bed. Soon she is snoring peacefully. Volodya sits down to scrape the mud off her boots. I take my leave.

Although my mother forbids me to visit Granny I like to call on her. I sit on the wooden bench by her door and wait for her to come back from the market. She stops at the gate, looking at me tenderly with a jug of her famous milk clutched to her breast. "Ah, shit of my shit, when you're a big boy you'll give your old Granny three kopecks for her hair-of-the-dog."

My grandmother is very good-natured when sober. She never bothers me about my homework or my performance at school; she's simply sure that I do better than all the rest. When I tell her about my quarrels with my stepfather she curses him and my mother but she doesn't approve of my attempts to run away. She always sends me back home at night.

Perhaps it is because of Granny that I like neither drinking nor drunks.

***

My first drinking party is on New Year's Eve at Victor's house. We lay out a feast of bread and herring and prepare ten litres of home-brew from sugar I filch from home. Someone brings a bottle of vodka. Victor's parents watch our preparations with amusement. The next day we feel so terrible we don't want to repeat the experiment for a long time.

By the time I reach fifteen I've been drunk no more than a dozen times. I don't yet have the taste for alcohol, though I will join my friends if they're drinking. Besides, it's unwise to come home with spirits on my breath because I have an informer sleeping in my room. Marusya is our home-help. A country girl who can barely read or write, she was born during the famine of 1920 when babies ran the risk of being stolen and butchered by their starving neighbours. But Marusya survived both the famine and collectivisation. When war broke out she escaped her farm by going to work in a munitions plant. There was a shortage of labour so they didn't ask for her passport.[4] Marusya poured mustard gas into shells on a conveyor belt. A partition separated the workers, so that an exploding shell would kill

---

4   Peasants had no passports, so that they were effectively tied to their collective farms.

only one person. You don't have to be literate to understand the dangers of such a job and Marusya was happy to come to work for my parents. Smallpox has blinded her in one eye and left her face pitted and scarred. I call her Cyclops.

With peasant cunning Cyclops notices that I have no one on my side, so she tries to ingratiate herself with my mother by getting me into trouble. But she goes too far when she accuses me of stealing her purse. My mother tells her to be careful.

"My son may be a hooligan but he's not a thief."

A few minutes later Cyclops is feigning surprise at finding her purse under a pile of clothes.

"As I went out in the summer morn to see my lover off to war…" she sings as she makes pies. I snigger at the thought of that old maid having a lover. The phone rings. Cyclops thunders out of the kitchen shouting "I'm coming!" as though the caller can hear her. It is Uncle Volodya for me.

"Come to the football match this afternoon. Bersol are playing Kuibyshev Metallurgists."

I meet Volodya at the triumphal entrance arch to Chapaevsk's stadium. It has no stands and no fence separating spectators from the pitch. The teams play with as much gusto as we boys do. Everyone throws himself into the attack and no one bothers about defence. Just before full time a penalty is awarded to the Kuibyshev side. The spectators rush onto the pitch and stand around the penalty area yelling abuse at the striker. It works. The shot is so weak our keeper saves it with ease. The referee tries to clear the pitch but the crowd threatens to turn him into soap and someone punches him.

Volodya and I stream happily away from the ground with the other men and boys. Some are taking nips from bottles stuffed into their pockets. The autumn air smells of damp birch leaves and bonfires. Smoke rises from bathhouses by the river where people are making *samogon*.

We run into Victor who produces a bottle of *Spirol* from his pocket. This is an alcohol-based medication that is rubbed on the head to cure dandruff. You can buy it cheaply at any chemists. Like many local men, Victor's father drinks *Spirol*. He also knows prison recipes for preparing alcohol from paint-thinner, furniture polish and glue.

Volodya refuses the *Spirol* and goes home to look after his mother. It's her drinking day. Victor and I tackle the bottle. The oily potion tastes disgusting, making me want to throw up. But at the same time a warm feeling spreads through my head and chest. I feel invulnerable. "Victor! I know why people drink!" I burst out laughing and think I'll never stop.

***

Dobrinin watches me like an eagle, waiting for an excuse to explode. My mother and sister eat in heavy silence. Unable to bear the tension any longer, I balance my knife on the salt pot and spin the blade. Dobrinin leaps to his feet, banging the table with his fist.

"You see! You see that little bastard?" he turns to my mother, "I feed him, put shoes on his feet… Get out! Leech!"

I run out of the house to my friend Gelka Kazin's. I hope he'll have enough for a bottle of *Spirol* or *Blue Danube*, but that day he has other things on his mind.

"Vanya, I have to get away from this damned place. The neighbours say Ma's a prostitute, just because men come here. I'm always getting into fights over it."

Gelka has no father. To make ends meet his mother takes in

sewing. She mends jackets and runs up shirts and trousers so it shouldn't be surprising that men come to her room. People in the barracks can't live without gossip.

Gelka's mother is always kind to me. When she comes in I tell her about my trouble with Dobrinin.

"Of course he's only my stepfather. My real father is working as a secret agent in a capitalist country. He's not allowed to contact us."

I still hope that he'll turn up one day, when the judges in Moscow realise their mistake. Or perhaps Stalin himself will hear of the miscarriage of justice and grant him a pardon.

"Oh they must have shot him years ago," says Gelka casually.

"No!" I make a headlong rush at Gelka, forgetting that he is our school boxing champion. He pushes me back into the corner. His mother leaps up and slaps his face.

"Get out!" she screams. "Take no notice, Vanya. I'm sure your father is doing valuable and patriotic work." She speaks firmly, but she has tears in her eyes.

Gelka and I patch things up and decide to leave town together. We'll become sailors. Grandfather Dobrinin writes to the Moscow naval ministry for a prospectus of all the academies in the USSR. We decide the Archangelsk academy will suit us best. It is on the open sea, unlike Baku or Astrakhan, and will be cheaper to reach than Vladivostock. Most important, we know that there'll be less competition than for Odessa or Leningrad. A top student in Chapaevsk is not the same as a top student in Moscow.

My parents tell me not to be in a hurry to leave, but I'm sure they'll sigh with relief when I finally walk out of the door.

2

Siberia

The 1950s

"How well he plays the balalaika!" we shout as the boy from Tula wakes up, howling and shaking his hands. Gelka slipped lighted strips of paper between his fingers while he slept.

Boys from all over the country have come to the Archangelsk Naval Academy to sit the entrance exams. Our dormitory is as noisy as a stack of nesting gulls. Gelka and I team up with three lads from Chelyabinsk to guard each other at night.

After our exams we wander the wooden streets of Archangelsk waiting for our results. Although I do well in the exams the Academy rejects me. My father is an Enemy of the People, and that is on my records. The navy does not want me in its ranks.

Term starts and we have to leave the Academy. My friends and I find an abandoned sea hunter moored near a timber yard. We move in, building bonfires on deck, drinking vodka, baking potatoes and singing pirate songs far into the night. In the daytime we earn cash loading wooden planks on the docks. When the police turn up we explain we're waiting for money from home. They leave us alone. Gelka's mother wires his return fare and he goes back to Chapaevsk. I'm determined to avoid that fate. I've tasted freedom for the first time since running away to the Front with Slavka.

Snow begins to fall. It is too cold to stay on our ship. I cross the Dvina to Solombala island, which is the real port of Archangelsk, and find a place in a seaman's hostel.

"There are foreign sailors here," the hostel's Party instructor tells us. "You must be very careful. If anyone from a capitalist country approaches you, report it immediately. Do not pick up anything you see in the streets. *Agents provocateurs* put chocolates and attractive magazines in bins so that they can take photos of Russians rummaging through rubbish."

I wonder if our newspaper photos of American scavengers are taken in the same way.

Despite the warnings we nod and grin at the foreign sailors. Mainly Norwegians, they're simple lads like us, interested in drinking and girls.

I come across *The Wave*, a pre-revolution coal ship, in dry dock in Solombala and on an impulse ask the skipper to take me on as ship's boy. I'm not yet sixteen but I plead my love for hard work and the sea. In the end he agrees. A few days later we set sail down the Dvina, bound for Spitzbergen.

"When will we see the sea?" I keep asking.

"Your father will reach the gates of hell first, lad," the sailors laugh, "don't be in a hurry."

As we cross the Arctic Circle my shipmates baptise me in a tub of sea water. The cold takes my breath away but they revive me with tumblers of vodka.

The Barents sea is always choppy. Water sprays onto the ship and freezes. From morning till night I break ice on the deck, spars and rigging. The worst task is cleaning up after coal has been loaded. The sailors like their ship to shine so I have to swill coal-dust off the decks and then wash it out of every nook and cranny with the point of a wet cloth. The incessant rain soaks my oilskins and weighs me down as I work.

"If you don't pull your weight, boy, you'll be off at the next port," the bosun growls. He turns to the other sailors: "Anyone who makes fun of this lad will get a punch in the face. Understood?"

We sail to the Spitzbergen port of Barentsburg, where there is a Soviet mining concession. Convicts work the mines. Barentsburg is foreign territory and therefore off-limits to a son of an Enemy of the People. When the other sailors have gone ashore for the evening I stand on deck looking at the stars and the lights from the port. Only the distant bark of a dog or a drunken shout breaks the silence. It seems that somewhere below the horizon a fire is burning, shooting flares into the heavens. Bars of green light stripe the sky, bending into weird forms. I feel sorry for the prisoners: their camp floodlights will blot out these northern lights.

Archangelsk is already cut off by the frozen White Sea so on our return voyage we unload our coal at Murmansk. The port is surrounded by logging camps. "Be vigilant," warns the *Wave*'s political instructor before we disembark. "The camps are full of criminals and Enemies of the People."

"Convicts slip letters between the logs," the bosun whispers to me. "Sometimes one of them cuts off a hand and nails it to a log. They hope that someone abroad will see it and make a fuss."

I've heard these camp stories before; they surprise me as little as night following day.

Our next voyage is to Igarka in Siberia. We sail via Franz Josef Land, taking supplies to the meteorologists who work on Rudolf Island in the far north of the archipelago. The shore is surrounded by ice floes which crash against each other so violently we can't land. We unload our cargo onto an ice sheet and the meteorologists come to fetch it on dog-sleds. They wave and shout greetings, happy to see their first visitors for months. I envy them. The Arctic seems exciting and romantic; people have only been living there for the short time I have been on this earth.

At the mouth of the Yenisei we take a navigator on board to steer us around the river's islands and shallows. We follow the river for hundreds of kilometres down to Igarka. Our political instructor again warns us to be vigilant as prisoners from the Norilsk camps work in the town. When I go ashore however, I find it hard to tell the difference between convicts and ordinary people. Some men come up and politely ask us to post letters for them so they can avoid the censor. We all agree. Later I drop four letters into a box in Archangelsk.

We sail back up the foggy Yenisei, through the Kara sea, and past the tip of Novaya Zemlya to Nar'ian Mar, where we have to deliver a *Victory* car to the local Party chief. The car drives us all mad. It gets in my way when I sweep the deck and its tarpaulin cover keeps wrenching loose and flapping like a dirty flag. When I try to fasten it down it resists me as though it were alive. Everyone is happy to see the last of the vehicle at Nar'ian Mar. It's a mystery where the Party boss will drive, for there are no roads in the region.

The *Wave* leaves me behind at Archangelsk. It's bound for the British Isles so they can't take me. The night it sails I go to a bar and get as drunk as a piglet's squeal. I wake up feeling sick but I have to get up and look for another post before the sea freezes over. As I drag myself out in the morning I see a sign in the hostel foyer: *Radio-operator training college in Riga seeks applicants. Fare paid.* I write and they accept me.

***

The boys travelling with me to Riga come from villages deep in the countryside. They've never seen a train before and are nervous of the iron horse. I laugh at the quaint way they speak: "Yesterday we were to a bar going, vodka drinking, with a soldier fighting."

The Riga train amazes us with its clean toilets and polite conductresses. There aren't even any cigarette butts on the floor. But beyond the window, war has left its traces in a desolate landscape of ruined buildings. We pass countless wrecks of German tanks. The people, in their grey padded jackets, look like the convicts of Igarka.

We can't afford restaurant car meals so we buy baked potatoes and cucumbers from old ladies on station platforms. Some potatoes are still raw in the centre. The country boys are shocked. It would never enter their heads to cheat in this way. People from the north are more honest than us, perhaps because they never had serfdom. In Central Russia people are still afflicted with the slave mentality and will try anything on if think they can get away with it, even when there's no point.

The outskirts of Riga are scarred with bombed factories; its centre is pitted with burned-out wooden buildings. We are surprised to find our college undamaged by war. It's a six-storey former hotel with *Anno 1905* embossed on its facade.

I quickly settle into the institute and soon enjoy the liking and respect of my fellows. The college is a friendly place. When a master punishes a boy by withholding his dinner the rest of us tip our dishes of porridge over the tables. Then we pick up our bread and walk out of the dining room. Perhaps not everyone wants to go along with this protest but they keep quiet in the face of our collective decision.

My best friend is a boy called Victor Rudenko. He comes from Kotlas, where his parents have been exiled as kulaks.[5] Victor has picked up criminal jargon and likes to show off by calling out to the other boys: "You over there with rickets!" or "You ugly bastard!"

Rudenko's bravado backfires, and he becomes known as 'Rickets.'

There are one or two petty dictators amongst the second year boys. Those of us who don't have the sense to keep out of their sight are constantly sent out for cigarettes or to take messages to girls at the bookbinders' college. I notice that some lads – most of them insecure boys from collective farms – actually enjoy this treatment. "For them life without servitude would be like life without cake," says Rickets.

Rickets and I make friends with a Rigan, Valerka Polenov. Valerka is small and his shoulders are raised as though shrugging in bewilderment. He dresses carelessly with his cap pulled down over one ear. His hero is Lord Byron. Half the time Valerka is in a different world. He's not even aware that people respect him. I never found out how he ended up in our college; he probably only comes because it's next door to his house.

Valerka's father is an administrator at the circus. In his spare time he makes records from x-ray films, engraving them with the songs of Vertinsky and Vadim Kozin. If you hold a disc up to

---

5   Kulaks were wealthy peasants who were shot or exiled to Siberia during the collectivisation period of the early 1930s.

the light you see a broken bone or vertebra. I drop in on Valerka's father to borrow some of these records. To reach the offices I have to walk through the circus dwarves' quarters. Seeing them close-up, I can't understand why we laugh at them. Without make-up, in the middle of their family quarrels, swearing, drinking and fighting, the dwarves are just like the people in our barracks at home. They are no different to anyone else; you might as well look in the mirror and laugh.

I like college, but the place where I really feel I belong – for the first time in my life – is the town's yacht club. When I see a notice in the papers appealing for new members I take a tram out to Lake Kish and present myself. They put me to work scraping paint and collecting rubbish. I throw myself into my tasks, hoping that my dedication to the job will prove my love for the sea. Everyone is busy preparing for the summer, cleaning and painting their yachts, which look like fragile, pretty toys. The friendship of the club is different to that of the institute; you don't have to use your fists to win respect.

When he finds out about my visits to the yacht club our college director phones to tell them I am skipping lessons. He must know I'm jumping the tram to get there and so he wants to stop me going. The club tells me they're sorry to lose me and that I should come back in a year's time.

I am furious, but there is nothing I can do without being expelled from the institute. After that I fill up my spare time by drinking with Rickets. The institute's political instructor warns us that the town is full of bourgeois elements and the older boys say that the Latvian Forest Brotherhood has been known to catch lone Russians and strangle them. Despite these warnings, Rickets and I take every opportunity to slope off together through the dark streets. A stroke of luck secures us an evening job unloading potatoes from railway wagons, so we have cash to spend. We usually go to the *Reindeer Antlers,* a back-street joint popular with soldiers and sailors. Walking down the steps and throwing open the door of the little basement bar is like crossing into another world, one of warmth and comradeship.

I mix my cocktail of vodka, beer, salt, pepper, mustard and vinegar. "Down the hatch!" I empty the glass in one. I learned to do this back in Chapaevsk by watching my friends' parents. I practised with water until I mastered the technique.

Regular fights break out in the *Reindeer Antlers,* but are usually stopped before serious injury occurs. Not to be outdone, Rickets and I fight each other at least once a month. It's a ritual between us and means nothing. Other customers try to pull us apart but the harder they try the more tightly we grapple with each other. Finally we stagger back up the basement steps and roll home with our arms about each other, roaring pirate songs into the damp night air.

The rich kids of Riga call themselves *stilyagi.* They listen to jazz and dance the boogie-woogie. They wear tight trousers and jackets with shoulder-pads as wide as the Pacific Ocean. I like western music too but these *stilyagi* are spoilt brats. You have to have a father in Party headquarters or a mother in a department store to dress as they do. The Komsomol paper denounces the *stilyagi* as 'spittle on the mirror of our socialist reality'; we just beat them up whenever we get the chance. They're pampered kids and useless at fighting.

In summer we are sent out from the college to work on the *Beria* collective farm. I've never seen such dereliction and misery. The mud is even worse than at home. There's no mechanical farm equipment; only worn-out horses. Our overseer spends his days drinking with the farm chairman. We sleep on straw in a shed and share the farmers' meals of potatoes and rye bread which is half raw and full of chaff. We skive off to help old people and single women with their private plots in return for food and home-brew. Samogon is the only consolation of farm life. Everyone distils it so no one denounces their neighbour. Besides, the local policeman is a villager too.

I can't understand why people live on this hopeless farm, why they don't run off wherever the wind blows. I am so relieved when our forced labour ends and we return to college that I don't even miss the constant supply of alcohol.

***

Did you cry when Stalin died? Does the world seem different now? writes Olga, one of my former classmates in Chapaevsk, in a letter to me that March. Stalin's death in 1953 produces an odd feeling in us all. For some reason everyone starts to speak in whispers, as though his corpse were lying in the next room. I take my place in the guard of honour by his portrait. We assemble in the sports hall to listen to the funeral broadcast. Some boys cry. I feel sad too and strangely insecure. Then Rickets starts a game of push and shove in the back row and I cheer up.

We are being prepared for work in remote Siberian stations where there won't be any phone connections. We'll have to know how to repair our equipment when it breaks down. The more they tell us about the difficulties that lie ahead the prouder we feel of our profession. We look down on boys from other colleges; aren't there already millions of fitters and lathe operators in this world?

For once in my life, everything seems to be going well. It's my final spring at the college. Then, unannounced, they decide to hold a room search and find a banned book among my things. The book is nothing special, just a dry work on atavistic memory lent to me by Valerka's mother who is a librarian at the Academy of Sciences. Nevertheless, I am summoned to the director's office.

"Where did you get this book?" the director bangs his fist on the desk. "Who gave it to you? I demand you tell me! Do you want to be expelled?"

My head spins. I don't know what to do. I am honour-bound to return the book to Valerka. On an impulse I snatch it from the director's hand and run out of the room. I give Valerka back his book. It would look bad for the college if I was expelled for reading banned literature so I escape with a reprimand.

The following Saturday I'm chatting to some girls from the bookbinder's college when our new teaching assistant comes up. "Got any more subversive literature?" he asks me. Turning to the girls he says: "Our Ivan here really caused a scandal last week."

"It's none of your business!" I shout.

He laughs.

"Okay you bastard," I swing a punch at him. I've already had a few beers and don't stop to consider that the assistant is twice my size. He knocks me to the ground as easily as if I had been a flea.

"Take him away, lads," he says to some of my classmates who have gathered to watch the fight. They pick me up and carry me off to my room. I remember that Rickets and I have hidden a bottle of vodka in his locker. I start the bottle by myself. The more I drink the worse I feel. Rickets still doesn't return, and before I know it I've finished the bottle. Some boys appear at the door and begin to tease me. I fling the empty bottle at them, then climb onto the window-ledge and jump.

The ground slams into me. I can't breathe. I lie with my face in the cobblestones. I'll keep still for a couple of minutes. It will give the others a fright. The smell of vomit fills my nostrils. I twist my neck to see one of my classmates throwing up in the gutter. I wonder why he's doing that. Perhaps he can't hold his drink.

"Don't move, Vanya, we've called an ambulance," says another boy in a shaky voice.

As they heave me onto a stretcher I catch sight of the teaching assistant. His face is pale.

"Excuse me for causing all this trouble," I grind out the words with heavy sarcasm.

The ambulance drive to the hospital seems endless. Thirst sears my mouth all night. I scream and curse until I pass out on the x-ray table.

I come to in agony and confusion. Both my legs and my right arm are covered in plaster. I have a vague impression that my mother has been near me.

"Well, young man," says the doctor, "you have eighteen fractures and your right kidney is damaged. It seems you broke your fall on some telegraph wires and that saved your life. Your mother was here. She stayed until we knew you were out of danger."

I don't want to live. Four shots of morphine a day barely help. I pleaded with a God I don't believe in to grant me a break from the relentless pain for even five minutes. I can't face the endless hours ahead, knowing there'll be no respite until nightfall when the nurse brings my sleeping tablets. With a great effort of will I manage to save some of these tablets and store them until I have 14. Then I swallow them all at once. They resuscitate me and pump my stomach. After that a nurse watches as I take my medicine.

I stop eating. They rouse my appetite with wine bought with money the college has sent in for my food. When the money runs out they give me diluted surgical spirit.

My arm and left leg begin to heal and they remove the cast but the pain in my right leg intensifies until it pulsates in violent waves through my whole body. I plead with the doctors to take the plaster off. They ignore me: "It's just the cast squeezing."

When they finally remove it they discover that pus has eaten away the cartilage around my knee.

My doctor, Professor Jaegermann, won't listen to my pleas to amputate my leg. He keeps draining the knee. It has swollen to the size of a football, while I can circle my upper thigh with my fingers.

I like morphine. It seems to wrap my pain in cotton wool and hold it at a distance, at least for a while. I ask for shots both before and after my dressings are changed but after a while they say I'm taking too much and refuse to give me any more. My pleas fall on deaf ears. An old French ward sister tells me that some of my shots were nothing more than saline solution. I send them all to hell and sulk, but I realise that if I've managed without morphine before I can do so in future.

I begin to mix with the other patients and my spirits lift. "Let's see the champion of jumping without a parachute," the TB sufferers say as they cluster round my bed to breathe in the smoke from my cigarettes. The men crack jokes and share cakes and vodka that their wives have sent in.

I sit up and do exercises. Professor Jaegermann tells me I'll never be able to bend my leg again but I will eventually be able to walk without crutches.

A few months later I get an order to go out to work in Primorskii Krai. That's beyond Vladivostock I am relieved.

I want to bury myself in the taiga far away from human eyes. My friends have already left for their Siberian posts. Valerka went to Yakutia. I hear that Rickets fell under a tram in Omsk. His injuries were worse then mine and he was sent back to his parents. That is the last I hear of him.

***

The Moscow-Vladivostock express is packed with labour recruits[6] desperate to make their pile of gold in the East. Some have spent years in prison camps; others are escaping collective farms. Old hands brag about the fortunes they've made in logging or mining and the adventures they had drinking up their pay.

By the time we reach Kazan we are on first name terms and sharing our food. Like every carriage on every long distance train in the country, ours has its joker, its card-trickster, its storyteller, and its drinkers. We're even blessed with a pair of newlyweds. The husband Mitya is an unpleasant young Komsomol activist, so possessive of his wife that he forbids her to alight at stops to stretch her legs. His bride Lena doesn't seem suited to him at all and we wonder what could have brought about their union.

It turns out that Mitya and Lena were at medical school together in Voroshilovgrad. When they graduated they were posted to Sakhalin, an island so distant it almost touches Japan. Lena has never been away from home before and she was afraid to travel such a long way by herself, so she took Mitya as her husband and protector.

A young sailor in our carriage takes a fancy to Lena. He confides in me as we stand smoking in the little space between

---

6 Labour recruits were offered bonuses to work in Siberia for a minimum of one year.

carriages: "Ivan, do me a favour and set up a game of chess with Mitya. I want to have a word with his wife."

The sailor lures Lena into the smoking compartment where he drips words of honey and poison into her ear. They seem to work, for the clandestine affair continues through western Siberia and along the Amur. Lena probably doesn't even notice Lake Baikal or the bust of Stalin carved into a mountain near Amazar. The rest of us do our best to keep the unsuspecting Mitya occupied.

Finally Lena makes up her mind. At Khabarovsk she hides in the next carriage with her sailor while Mitya alights alone. He weeps as he sorts out his belongings. I almost feel sorry for him. Still, no doubt he'll forget Lena as he forges his Party career.

When we reach Vladivostock I say goodbye to Lena and her sailor. As I watch them walk away through the station I wonder if her suitor will live up to his promises. Then I put on my rucksack and catch a tram to the Central Meteorological Office.

They send me to work as second radio operator aboard the *Franz Mehring*. We sail to weather stations around the Sea of Okhotsk, bringing food, kerosene and alcohol. This spirit is 95 degrees proof, for normal vodka freezes in the Siberian cold. Drunk neat or mixed with a handful of snow, it's the hardest currency in the region. A bottle gets you anything you want. At each station the meteorologists greet us like long-lost relatives and together we toast our arrival.

***

The station at Khaningda has been silent for a year. Not expecting to find anyone there, we're astonished to see a woman waving to us from the shore as we approach. The woman is hysterical. We give her vodka to calm her but every time she opens her mouth she weeps. She has a young daughter with her. We take them aboard and tell them they'll get medical care at Okhotsk.

As we sail the woman, whose name is Marina, recovers enough to tell her story: "At the beginning of autumn three men arrived. They said they were fishermen who'd lost their net. We let them into the station but they had knives... they spared me and my daughter Anna. They had escaped from a Kolyma camp. They smashed the radio equipment, ate our food and made spirits from our sugar. They forced me to cook for them; they threatened to kill Anna if I didn't.

"Vladivostock sent a rescue party, but the convicts saw it in the distance. They took us with them into the taiga and waited. The rescuers found our station abandoned and went away again.

"When the spring thaw came the convicts set off across the taiga to a railhead. They took most of the food stores with them, leaving us only potatoes and dried fish. Thank God neither Anna nor I fell ill."

As Marina tells her story Anna sits in deep shock. She stares at us with frightened eyes, not moving a muscle.

At Okhotsk we learn that the convicts who held Marina and Anna prisoner at Khaningda finally gave themselves up. Defeated by the taiga, they begged to be allowed back to camp.

After reloading we sail south to Shikatan in the Lesser Kurile islands. The port is inhabited by a colony of women who process catches of fish from the Sea of Okhotsk and the Pacific Ocean. Some are labour recruits; others are former prisoners from the Kolyma camps. Conditions there are almost as bad as in the camps: the women live in bleak barracks and their clothes are always wet and filthy. Their lives consist of working, drinking and fighting.

I want to go ashore to find a bar at Shikatan, but we're advised to stay on board ship. They tell us sailors have been sexually assaulted by gangs of women who roam the town at night.

On its return voyage the *Franz Mehring* puts me ashore at Adimi point. I am to go inland to work as a radio operator at the village of Akza. An Udege[7] called Viktor Kaza joins me, with a couple of meteorologists who are travelling even further into the taiga. We put our belongings on a horse and cart and set off on foot. I never dreamed it would be so hard to walk on crutches. Towards the end of the day I'm exhausted and throw away my heavy coat. Without a word Viktor goes back to fetch it for me.

Our first stopping-place, Samarga, is a miserable collection of moss-covered wooden huts strung out across an isthmus within a bend of the river. There's a fishing collective, an elementary school and a hospital. The buildings are raised on stone piles to protect them from flooding. Long tables for gutting fish stand outside. The debris is eaten by gulls or washed away by storms. The air stinks of rotten fish. I used to think the cries of sea-birds romantic, but in Samarga they remind me of the drunken beggar-women on Chapaevsk trains.

The fast-flowing Samarga river takes great skill to navigate. Victor Kaza arranges for a fellow Udege, Shurka the Grouse-Catcher, to guide us upstream. However Shurka is busy drinking up his pay from a previous voyage and a week passes before he's sober enough to steer a boat again. Eventually we set out in an *ulmaga*, a long boat made from a hollowed tree-trunk. Its prow is flattened into a shovel-shape so that it glides over submerged rocks. At waterfalls we climb out and walk upriver while Shurka and his son carry the boat on their shoulders.

---

7 The Udege are a Siberian people who live on the eastern seaboard of the Primorye region. In the 2002 census they numbered 1,657. They were nomadic hunters until forcibly settled in the 1930s.

Shurka the Grouse-Catcher punts the boat from the prow while his wife paddles from the stern. Their son lies on the floor of the boat sucking lump sugar. I fear that at any instant the *ulmaga* will overturn or be split by a rock. Shurka deploys great skill in keeping it head-on into the current; if he misjudges an angle the boat will swing around and be swept off downstream.

Back in Samarga I watched Shurka sign his contract with us. The sweat stood out on his forehead as he struggled to steer a pencil across the paper. Yet with a boat-pole in his hand he's a virtuoso, reading the river like a book. Unbothered by midges, he takes advantage of every break to catch fish or shoot grouse.

When we reach our destination Shurka comes to me in a temper because he had some money deducted from his pay 'as a tax on childlessness.'

"I've got eleven children."

"You have to fill in a form," I explain.

He stares at me in astonishment.

"Don't worry, I'll fill in your forms for you. Here, let's toast Dalstroi."[8]

I open a bottle of vodka and Shurka calms down.

Akza is a cluster of 20 huts, an elementary school, a shop and a medical post. The clubhouse burned down the year before. A few dozen Udege and nine Russians live in the village. A man from Leningrad named Kryuchkov has been here since 1924. After graduating from university he contracted TB. The doctors advised him to leave Leningrad's damp and foggy atmosphere. Every Udege family in Akza has a child who resembles Kryuchkov.

Dr Yablonsky is also from Leningrad. Once he was head of

---

8 Dalstroi was the collective name of the northern Siberian camps.

a university department and spoke four languages but he was exiled during the purge of the Leningrad intelligentsia.[9] Now Yablonsky has the shaking hands and watery eyes of an alcoholic. He forgot his European languages long ago and learned Udege in their place.

A third Russian is Pasha Dyachkovsky, a skilled hunter with luxuriant curving moustaches. He's married to a local Udege woman, Duzga. Kryuchkov warns me that when drunk Pasha wets his bed and then he beats his wife mercilessly.

A few days after my arrival we gather for a drink to celebrate Pasha's birthday. After a while he feels the urge to urinate. He rises from the table, grabs Duzga and starts pulling out her hair in clumps like carrots. We leap up to restrain him but this offends his soul to the core. He goes home, barricades himself in, climbs up to the attic with his gun and takes aim at anyone who comes within his field of vision. This is serious, as he lives above the shop which Duzga runs. We need to buy food. Fortunately for us, the next day Pasha decides to go hunting in the taiga.

"He usually conquers his hangover this way," Dr Yablonsky explains.

There is very little to do in Akza apart from hunt and drink. I can't hunt because of my leg, so I make myself popular by filling in for the observers when they're out hunting or too drunk to work. Of course I drink too, but I have a good stomach for vodka. Even after two bottles I can tap out: 'The weather report from Akza is…'

***

It is evening and we've gathered for a drink. I grow excited. Leaping onto a chair I start to declaim some of Yesenin's poems.

---

9   This purge began after the murder of Kirov in 1934.

"Do any of you understand these lines?" I shout. "Buried out here in the taiga you've never known the world he describes – or you've already forgotten it."

The next day it occurs to me that Kryuchkov has seen Yesenin in the flesh. I realise I should apologise to him, but somehow I can never bring myself to do so. After that I keep out of Kryuchkov's way, hanging back if I see him enter the shop ahead of me.

On my day off I pack a bottle, a book and some food in my rucksack and walk into the taiga. I stop beneath a tree, open my bottle and settle down to read. But my attention wanders, caught by the loveliness of my surroundings. I never imagined that this earth could be so beautiful. I am surrounded by hills clothed in larch and cedar. Where there has been a fire and the trees have not yet grown back the slopes are covered in brilliant red flowers. Now I have no regrets that I've left 'civilisation.'

The other Russians do not share my enthusiasm. When I praise the beauty of the taiga to Pasha he snaps: "Go and play in the dirt you young wipe-snot," and strides off.

For the first time in my life I have my own room. It contains a stove and a camp bed. A door from the burned-down club serves as a table with blocks of wood for stools. The pile of deerskins I sleep on is as soft as a feather-bed. I mention to Victor Kaza that I need cooking utensils. "Come with me," he says, and leads me out into the taiga. In a small clearing we come upon a larch which has been festooned like a Christmas tree with aluminium spoons, pans and pieces of cloth.

"In my grandfather's time we laid the dead person in an *ulmaga* and hung it from the tree," says Victor. "We put berries and salted mushrooms in the boat. The dead had everything they needed for their journey into the next world."

Victor unties a frying pan and gives it to me. I feel a little sorry for him as he is a misfit among the other Udege. His hunchback prevents him from hunting and he tries to compensate for this by flaunting his seven years' schooling. This is useless as the Udege value hunting far more highly than literacy. Victor has a mentally-retarded Russian wife. I don't know how she ended up at Akza but it's obvious she's been in a labour camp.

"Lyuba you haven't put your knickers on," Pasha cries as she passes by.

Lyuba grins and lifts the hem of her skirt over her head to reveal bright crimson bloomers. We all laugh at her until Victor emerges from their hut.

"Lyuba, pull your *chemise* down," he pulls her indoors. The watching Udege roar with laughter again, this time at Victor's pretensions.

February comes round and the entire settlement gives itself up to an orgy of drunkenness. The occasion is the pelt-collector's annual visit. This man is Tsar, God and high court judge rolled into one. He rides up the frozen Samarga to buy furs, accompanied by horse-sleighs laden with goods for Duzga's shop.

The pelt-collector brings enough cash to pay three or four hunters. This is the only time of the year that the Udege see money, although they sometimes earn a little by guiding geologists or doing some building work. They go to the pelt-collector one by one, beginning with his relatives and drinking partners. No one dares cross him or he'll refuse to buy their 'soft gold,' which is a state monopoly. After a day or two the collector takes back the money that the hunters have spent in Duzga's shop. With this cash he pays the next group. This process lasts till all the hunters' pay is in Duzga's pocket and from there, of course, it goes back to the state.

The Udege drink for days on end, quietening their babies with rags soaked in vodka. A few women have the foresight to take cash from their husbands' pockets to buy flour, sugar, salt and dress material. The rest have to spend the year humbling themselves before Duzga, who gives credit because she enjoys having people in her debt. She's the most powerful person in Akza and you have to take care not to make an enemy of her. When they've drunk all their pay the Udege go to sleep. A few days later the men emerge with their guns and head out into the taiga again.

An old Udege known as Grandad Chilli drops in on me unannounced. I bustle about trying to make him comfortable, brushing cigarette butts and paper off a stool. He sits smoking roll-ups in silence. After half an hour he rises and walks out without a word. I'm worried, thinking that I might have done something to offend him. I don't want to cross Grandad Chilli for I know he once killed a Russian teacher out of jealousy. When the police came for him he disappeared into the taiga for a long time. No one in the village denounced him.

I tell Dr Yablonsky about the old man's behaviour. "Don't worry," he reassures me, "the Udege only speak when they want to sell you something or buy vodka. That was simply what they call 'paying a visit.' He must like you. If you ask him he'll show you his piece of quartz that has a seam of gold in it as thick as a finger. Last year he showed it to some geologists who were passing through here. He said he knew a place where there were many more like it. They hired him as a guide in return for as many cans of condensed milk as could drink. He led them by the nose for a few weeks until finally he confessed he had forgotten the place. They went back to the coast and now he's waiting for more prospectors this summer. The Udege know what'll happen if geologists find gold in the region."

After that I feel more comfortable with the taciturn Udege. We Russians are supposed to be civilized, and yet we waste so much effort on words which are at best empty and at worst cruel and deceptive.

In summer the clubhouse is finally repaired, and to mark the occasion Samarga sends up the film *The Age of Love* with Lolita Torres. For once the Udege show excitement, even bringing babes-in-arms and their beloved dogs to watch. The projectionist is drunk and mixes up the reels, but no one notices.

I'm hoping to save some money during my posting in the East but it proves impossible. As soon as I receive my pay I go over to Duzga to stock up on vodka. I decide to move to Yuge, the most remote station in the Primorye region. There is nowhere to spend money in Yuge so my wages will be saved for me in Samarga.

I set off with a convoy of sledges bringing the annual delivery of post and supplies. As there is a severe frost we all have a good drink before we leave and top up along the way. I can't walk over the rugged terrain so I'm strapped onto a sledge. As it mounts an incline my horse stumbles and falls, dragging my sledge after it. The horse breaks its leg and has to be shot. The sledge rolls on top of me, leaving me grazed but otherwise unhurt, or so I think. They give me vodka and tie me to another sledge. By the time we reach that night's resting place I've sobered up enough to realise that I have broken my leg. In the morning they send me down to hospital in Samarga.

The hospital has neither electricity nor plaster of Paris. It's staffed by a doctor, a nurse and a medical assistant called Ivan Ivanich, who drinks continually out of homesickness. In the morning Ivan Ivanich's hands shake so badly I have to light his cigarettes for him. The doctor refuses to let him help reset my leg. While the nurse shoves a phial of ether under my nose the doctor presses on my leg with all her strength. I pass out.

When I come round I see the two women lying unconscious on the floor. The inexperienced nurse must have inhaled the ether herself and somehow given the doctor a whiff of it too. My leg has to be put in splints again. It grows back curved like a sabre from hip to ankle.

My deformity makes me horribly self-conscious. I had been thinking it was time I got married but now my hopes are dashed. I can't imagine any normal woman wanting to marry a man with a leg like mine and I don't want to end up with a wife like Victor's Lyuba.

HQ offers to send me to the coast but after all I've suffered I want to be as far from civilisation as possible. I insist on going to Yuge, so they send me up again on a sledge and I begin work there.

In Yuge I learn that insects truly are the scourge of the taiga. Our observation station is full of bugs and the grass outside crawls with encephalitis ticks. Each time I cross the threshold of my hut I have to strip off and examine myself from head to foot. Down by the river where there's little wind the midges surround me in clouds, biting straight through gauze into my skin. They make mosquitoes seem as harmless as butterflies. The only way to live in the taiga is to be like Shurka the Grouse-Catcher and take no notice of midge bites.

Winter comes as a relief, but by now my tobacco has run out.

I nearly go insane. Thoughts of cigarettes fill my days and my dreams at night. I pull out all the butts that have fallen between floorboards. I remember a place near the river where I tossed a half-smoked cigarette three weeks ago. When daylight comes I go out and fill a bucket with snow from that spot. I melt the snow on the stove and strike lucky, fishing out the soggy butt, drying and smoking it. I've never enjoyed a smoke so much in my life, but within ten minutes I'm prising up floor-boards again

I grow bored with life in the deep taiga. Work takes up no more than two or three hours a day and there is nothing to do for the rest of the time. There are no books. I even miss the society of Akza.

I start to think more and more about my pen friend Olga Vorobyova in Chapaevsk. We've been corresponding since my college days. Olga is a pretty, down-to-earth girl. Most importantly, when I write to her about my leg she doesn't seem to be bothered. Her letters are full of questions about my plans for the future. I begin to think about returning to a normal life. Perhaps I'll ask Olga to marry me. With the money I've saved here I'll be able to rent a room so we won't have to live with our parents.

My three-year posting comes to an end, much to my relief. I leave for Vladivostock, saying say goodbye to my acquaintances in Akza – those that are left. Yablonsky has been rehabilitated and returned to Leningrad. I never manage to apologise to Kryuchkov. With the first signs of spring he died, as TB sufferers often do.

I reach Samarga and collect 120,000 roubles in pay. This is a fabulous sum. Back home it would take a factory worker several years to earn that amount. I stay in Samarga for two weeks waiting for the sea-route to open. The shop has run out of vodka but there's a good supply of champagne. When he goes home for dinner the shopkeeper locks the medical assistant Ivan Ivanich and me in the shop and we continue to work through the bottles. In the evening we count the empties and I pay. There's no other way to pass the time. The local women don't appeal to me: after years of fish-gutting their buttocks sag so low they have to lift them up with their hands when they want to sit down.

In the morning before the shop opens I chat to the shopkeeper's paralysed son. He listens open-mouthed to my tales of Riga and Moscow.

"But why do they build the houses so tall?" he keeps repeating. "Why do people want to live on top of each other?"

My hair hasn't been cut for three years and local kids follow me around, jeering as though I'm some sort of hermaphrodite. My first stop in Vladivostock is a barber's. After I've cleaned up I go to a restaurant and soon I'm sending bottles to every table. I'm overjoyed to be back in civilisation again and spend a riotous month celebrating the event. At least I have the foresight to buy my ticket home before I blow all my wages. I arrive back in Chapaevsk with a blinding hangover and 68 roubles in my pocket.

3

Decembrists

The 1960s

"Goosie, goosie, goosie!"

"Hee, hee, hee!"

"Ten by three?"

"Me, me, me!"

My workmates and I emerge from the shower-room in troikas.[10] One man in each group runs off for a bottle while the other two go to order some snacks.

In the canteen we're held up by a woman from the shop floor who is already drunk and arguing with the server: "I asked for soup – what are these slops?"

"Push off, Zhenya, we want to get finished tonight," says the serving woman.

"What do you know about work? We're up to our knees in DDT all day."

"If you don't like the job go somewhere else."

"Someone has to do it."

"Get a move on ladies," shouts my drinking-partner, Lyokha-Tuba.

---

10 It was customary for a troika of three men to pool ten roubles to buy a bottle of vodka.

Zhenya rounds on him: "And what do you men know about hard work? You technicians sit around on your arses all day while we're getting ourselves in a sweat."

"With Igor Fyodorovich in your case," remarks the serving woman.

Everyone starts screaming, so Lyokha and I give up on bread and pickles and sit down to wait for our mate. He comes running in with the bottle, takes his seat and pours out three glassfuls. I raise mine: "To women."

"The trouble with this place," Lyokha remarks, "is that however long you spend in the shower you still come out smelling of DDT."

"Yeah, it makes me feel as though I'm crawling with lice,"[11] I say. "Never mind. We're the envy of the town for breathing in this crap all day long."

"But what's the use of getting higher pensions if we don't live long enough to enjoy them?"

"It could be worse. How many of those poor sods who made mustard gas before this place was converted are still alive?"[12]

"My mother does okay," I observe. "For a dose of Lewisite she trots off to a sanatorium in the Crimea each year."

"Funny how Party lungs are more sensitive than anyone else's," says Lyokha.

Lyokha's face and hands are coloured bright tomato-red, making him appear an even heavier drinker than he actually is. A couple of weeks ago a woman worker sprinkled potassium manganese on his head while he slept. When he stood in the

---

11 DDT was used to get rid of lice.

12 After the war, plants that had made chemical weapons were converted to pesticide production.

shower after work the powder dyed him a deep red. It's taking a long time to wash out and everyone laughs at him, especially the women.

That woman was getting her revenge on Lyokha for a trick he played on her. Night-shift workers like to take forty winks behind their gas masks. Last month Lyokha crept up as the woman slept and painted black ink over the goggles of her mask. Then he shook her awake, shouting: "Fire!" She awoke in terror and blindly leaped into the water tank. Unfortunately it was empty and she broke her arm. She couldn't complain because she shouldn't have been sleeping and besides, no one grasses on their fellow workers.

After we've drunk the bottle I put on my beret, sling my gas-mask container over my shoulder and say goodbye to my friends. I have a date with my former classmate and pen friend Olga Vorobyova.

Now that I'm back in Chapaevsk, Olga and I are talking of getting married. The problem is finding somewhere to live. The waiting list for a flat is twenty years. In the meantime I cannot live with my parents and I will not live with hers.

Olga works as a gynaecologist in a local clinic. That night she takes me out on her ambulance rounds, disguising me in a white coat. I'm interested to see the inside of other people's flats, although they all look alike. At midnight I strike lucky, for while Olga is attending an emergency I manage to pinch some morphine from her supply and inject myself. I haven't lost my taste for the drug.

***

The first months of our marriage are happy ones. We move into a flat of our own in Stavropol-on-the-Volga where communism has almost been built.[13] The Kuibyshev hydroelectric power project has flooded old Stavropol and convict labour is building a new town on the banks of the reservoir. I go over and find a job in a synthetic rubber factory. After three months the plant allocates us a flat and Olga comes to join me.

We live like everyone else, going with the flow like shit down the Yenisei. Our one-room flat has a toilet and running water. Olga's parents give us a table and a bed. After a year my factory presents us with a place on the waiting list for a washing machine.

My wife persuades me to take a course at a branch of Kuibyshev polytechnic in Stavropol. If I graduate I'll be able to leave the shop-floor and work in the plant's technical department. I prepare well for the entrance exams, going through a text-book of maths problems set by Moscow university. The evening before my exam we're invited to a neighbours' wedding and I drink more than I planned. My hands shake as I write the exam but I pass with a '4.' Afterwards I have a few pick-me-ups, quarrel with Olga, and meet some friends who take me to stay with them in their hostel until the row blows over. It would have been churlish to abuse my friends' hospitality by refusing a drink. I turn up for my next exam but can't hide the fact that I am drunk. I say straight out to the examiners: "Yes, I'm drunk, but I came here to sit my exams instead of having a hair-of-the-dog. Ask away, and if I get the answers wrong, fail me."

The strangest thing of all is that I pass. However, I fail the essays. By the time I sit these I'm quite incapable of writing.

---

13 The Kuibyshev dam and hydro-electric power plant, built by prison labour, were completed in the early 1960s and hailed by the government as 'the building of communism.' Stavropol-on-the-Volga was later renamed Toliatti after the Italian communist.

Of course I drink a bit, especially on payday which my workmates and I celebrate wherever we can. We usually go to the barracks where there are several single women who are glad of some company. As the night wears on one or two of the lads might wander off home but few can bear to leave their battle stations. Although none of us is exactly an enthusiast for front-rank Soviet labour, our conversation centres around work - there is little else to talk about.

Sometimes a wife turns up at the door, shouting and spoiling our party. Olga never humiliates herself this way, but she occasionally sends one of my more restrained friends to fetch me home.

Lyokha follows me to Stavropol. He finds a job at my plant, and he and his wife move into a flat in our block. One Sunday I come home to find a crowd gathered in our courtyard. I push my way through. Lyokha is standing on his balcony, wearing only his vest and long-johns. A horse stands beside him. I recognise it as the sad old mare who pulls the beetroot-cart to the grocery store below. Wild-eyed and dishevelled, Lyokha is yelling to his wife: "Masha, Masha, come here sweetie! I want to introduce you to this fine stallion. Perhaps he can satisfy you, my dear? You might refuse me but not him, surely?"

Lyokha's wife emerges from the building and takes off down the road like a startled hare. The crowd swell, shouting their encouragement as Lyokha delivers a drunken speech on his wife's coldness. The police arrive. The horse refuses to budge so the fire brigade have to be called to winch it down.

Lyokha is sent to prison camp and his wife moves in with a local policeman.

***

It takes a lot of vodka to make me drunk, so no one notices at work if I'm slightly the worse for wear. I start the day with a hair-of-the-dog, have a top-up at lunchtime and begin to drink in earnest in the evening. Vodka is my reward for a dangerous and boring job.

When the government passes a decree against drinking in factory canteens we produce our own spirit on the shop-floor. This 'syntec,' as we call it, is made by pumping air through buckets of triethylphosphate. The acidity of carbon dioxide in the air separates ethyl alcohol from the phosphoric acid. Holding our noses and closing our eyes against the fumes we knock back our syntec in the showers and then leave the plant before the full effect hits us.

In December a law is passed against public drunkenness. A boss, neighbour or relative can ring the police to report you. No further proof is needed. A whiff of alcohol on your breath is enough to get you locked up for 15 days. Alcoholics have become the new Enemies of the People. The thinking follows along these lines: a drunk 'damages his human worth,' so he should be locked up for the night in a special holding station, without medical help. After this he will take heart and emerge in the morning sober and ready to build our shining future. The cost of this service is knocked off his wages. That is the theory. In reality the police have to meet their targets of catching a certain number of drunks. They pick up anyone who has the slightest sniff of booze about them. They don't bother the hardened drunks in town; there's no point. They don't work, so there's nowhere to send the bill.

I am sentenced as a Decembrist[14] when a neighbour reports

---

14 Decembrists were revolutionaries sentenced in 1825 for plotting against Tsar Nicholas the First. In this context they were drunks sentenced according to the December laws.

me for banging on my door. I've lost my key and forgotten that Olga is at work. My trial lasts no more than a minute and the verdict is not subject to appeal. I do my time in a filthy police cell, deprived of tobacco and sleeping on the bare floor.

On my release I'm summoned to a workplace meeting and branded as a stain on the honour of the collective. Party demagogues and careerists have free rein. My mates sit solemnly through my denunciation, knowing that any one of them could be standing in my shoes. Afterwards they take me out for a consolation drink.

In an attempt to humiliate us Decembrists the plant erects a bottle-shaped booth and a metal cup by its gates. We are paid our wages through a little window in the side of the bottle. We have to stand in the cup while the entire workforce of the plant files past to the bus stop. Soon the bottle becomes a place where troikas assemble before running to the nearest vodka shop.

'To hell with them all,' I think as I sink even lower. I see no reason to stop drinking. Life will be no better without the bottle. Shops won't suddenly fill with goods and the people around me won't blossom into interesting companions. I find a thousand convincing reasons to get drunk. If the house is clean and tidy, that has to be toasted; if Olga nags me, I have to register my protest. If someone makes a rude or untrue remark about me, I drink to console my hurt feelings. Most often it's my wife who is guilty of wounding my soul.

Each time I overstep the mark I renounce the bottle for two or three months until my resolve crumbles. My periods of abstention convince me that I can leave the drink alone. Yet whether I am drinking or not I always have alcohol on my mind; I believe everyone has.

I miss so much work that my plant threatens the sack. Olga wants me to have treatment.

"I drink no more than anyone else," I protest

"Then why don't you spend less time with your drinking-partners and take a correspondence course? With a few qualifications you might get a more interesting position where you wouldn't want to waste all your time drinking."

"You must be mad if you think I'm going to spend my free time studying dialectical materialism. Just so I can swap my hammer and screwdriver for a phone and pen – and for what? To win the right to bark at my friends? Anyway, you're a 'professional' but you earn less than me no matter how many abortions you perform."

"I sometimes wonder why I married you."

"Because if you hadn't, you would have had to repay your debt to the state by going to practise your medical skills on some godforsaken collective farm. Not even your Party Papa could have saved you from that fate."

In the end I agree to seek treatment just to keep everyone quiet. Through her contacts Olga gets me into a psychiatric clinic. They give me three grams of a drug called Antabuse, followed by 30-40 grams of vodka. This cocktail takes my breath away. They revive me with oxygen and apomorphine, though not enough of the latter for my taste.

With Antabuse in my system I keep off the booze for eight months. Our daughter Natasha is born and I stay at home caring for her while my wife works night shifts.

***

In summer my family and I go to stay at the dacha at Studioni Avrag. The old folks are long dead but my Aunt Ira still lives there with her husband Dmitri Maslovski and their daughter. In the 1920s Uncle Dima inherited a large house in the centre of Kuibyshev. The upkeep proved too expensive so he sold it for the fabulous sum of half a million roubles. Thus the Maslovski family escaped poverty despite Uncle Dima's alcoholism.

One evening we discuss literature over dinner.

"Dostoevsky," I opine, "is old-fashioned. He uses too many words. In short, he's boring."

Uncle Dima goes to the bookshelves and pulls out a set of ten volumes. "These are for you, Vanya. Dostoevsky's collected works."

I read the books out of respect for my uncle, who was once rector of a college in Ukraine. They open my eyes: people in the last century lived their daily lives just as we do! If only Mitya Karamazov and Nastasya Filipovna were my brother and sister – how well we'd understand each other! What wild times we would have! The drunkard Marmeladov could be me! Remembering my childhood admiration for Robinson Crusoe, I wonder why people in books are so much more interesting than those in real life.

***

I slip four boxes of codeine into my socks and a hot-water bottle full of vodka into my waistband. Then I cross into the prisoners' zone where my old friend Lyokha is waiting at a pre-arranged spot. With a wink, he slips me some packets of sugar in return for my drugs. In town we don't see sugar for months on end, but the prisoners can buy it in their camp shop. On the other hand we can get as much codeine as we want from our chemists without a prescription.

I think Lyokha is unfortunate to have ended up behind barbed wire, but I feel no pity for the rest of the prisoners. They must have done something to earn their sentences, although I don't blame them when they skive off work. No one likes working under the lash. There's nothing to distinguish the prisoners from the rest of us except their shaven heads. We are warned to be vigilant but that is unnecessary for they keep to themselves.

About half the inhabitants of Toliatti are former zeks[15] who were freed when Khrushchev revised the Criminal Code in 1961. Ex-cons differ little from the rest of us. We all hate Party activists. Anyone who hob-nobs with the bosses is a traitor. Perhaps in Moscow shop-floor workers drink with engineers and administrators but in the provinces, the bosses are our enemies. Arse-lickers are shunned by their workmates, leaving them with nothing else to do but build their careers.

Lyokha is released after serving a year for hooliganism. Strangely enough, his wife leaves her policeman and returns to him. I ask Lyokha why.

"Simple, Vanya. My exceptional virility is instantly apparent to women, and not only to my wife, but doctors, singers, any woman at all. I only have to talk to a tractor for five minutes and it starts to run after me."

"Vanya," Lyokha calls one evening, "I'm on night-shift. Bring a bottle over to the office and get out of your wife's hair."

I'm only too happy to comply with his request. The local shop is already closed so I stop off at a flat where Gypsies trade around the clock.

Lyokha has taken a job as a phone engineer. I arrive at his office and we down the bottle between us. The vodka sets me free. I forget about my work, my wife and my leg. Just then it

---

15 *Zaklyuchonniye*: prisoners.

seems that no one understands me better than Lyokha.

"You know, Lyokha, I can't talk to Olga like I can to you. She is close to me, but after all, she is my wife. We know each other too well. I can guess what she's going to say even as she opens her mouth."

"I know. I stopped reading poems to Masha after I married her. But never mind, Vanya, listen to this," replies Lyokha, and hands me a set of headphones. He dials a number.

"It's the director of Plant No. 2," he explains.

When a man's voice answers Lyokha says politely: "This is the telephone maintenance collective. How long is your telephone cord?"

We hear the idiot waking his wife and sending her to fetch a tape measure.

"Two and a half metres."

"Very good. Now pull out the cord and stick it up your arse."

Lyokha and I double over with laughter and hang up. At three in the morning. Lyokha calls the director again and shouts down the line: "It's me! You can take it out now!"

Lyokha is soon dismissed from the phone collective. After that he returns to Chapaevsk, where he can only find work as a 'golden man,' as we call those who scoop shit out of the barrack latrines.

***

I meet Ivan Shirmanov at a works party. He surprises me by drinking nothing at all. I've met teetotallers before but there's nothing priggish about Ivan. He plays the accordion well and his anecdotes are unusually witty. I talk to him about my life in the Far East. He nods: "I know the taiga; I was in Kolyma."[16]

---

16 Kolyma was an area of camps in the Soviet Far East.

Ivan stops coming to work and our trade union sends me to find out what has happened to him. He lodges in a pre-revolution wooden house. His sister Elizaveta is reluctant to let me in but I persuade her I'm here to help. She ushers me into a gloomy, evil-smelling room. Empty bottles roll around the floor. Ivan lies on an iron bedstead; its mattress soaked through where he has wet himself.

"He needs a doctor, he can't stop drinking by himself," says his sister.

Ivan lies on his back, giggling like a mischievous schoolboy.

"Elizaveta, you poor woman. You don't know how amusing it is to see everything floating before your eyes. My thoughts are butterflies. So pretty, so fascinating… I'll catch that one. No wait, it's gone! Oh, the devils!"

Ivan has a fit of laughter.

"Ivan, what should I do? D'you want to keep your job?" I ask, "If you leave it any longer they'll dismiss you for 'dishonourable reasons' and then you'll be portering for the rest of your life."

In silence he hands me a notice of resignation that he has already written out.

"You don't have to resign. We can come up with an excuse."

Ivan remains unmoved: "I want to leave without a fuss. This is my problem. I must sort it out myself."

Next day I tell my workmates what has happened. They are a good bunch, none of them careerists or back-stabbers, and we decide to pack the next trade union meeting to plead Ivan's case. It is forbidden to dismiss someone without the approval of their union and unions have to have the agreement of their members. Ivan's dismissal is presented for approval. I speak up: "Comrades! Is it not our duty to help Comrade Shirmanov? As the advanced class the proletariat triumphed over the bourgeoisie, can we not also triumph over alcoholism, not that there is really any such thing in the USSR? Let us return Comrade Shirmanov to the right path!"

Strangely enough, the meeting is swayed by my argument and the union even proposes to pay my fare to escort Ivan to the mental hospital. A Party man, Sashka Akulshin, accompanies us. Sashka has left his family behind in Chapaevsk while he arranges accommodation in Stavropol. His absence from his wife and his no-less-beloved Party organisation leads him into strong temptation. When Ivan suggests going by bus instead of taxi Sashka readily agrees. After all, we're economising the money that the work collective has contributed to the return of the prodigal son. By the time we reach the clinic the doctors can't tell who is bringing in whom for treatment. I only recognise the hospital by the slogan on its outside wall: *Let us Wage War on Drunkenness!*

Despite our efforts Ivan never returns to work in our plant. He takes portering jobs and his sister continues to look after him. He is the only one of my friends my wife will lend money to, although she knows quite well what he wants it for.

"If I don't lend it to him poor Elizaveta will," she says.

One day Ivan and I go out in search of good beer. The only bar that sells it is on the steamer that plies between Moscow and Astrakhan. We board the boat, go to the restaurant and buy up all the beer they have. Then we sit back and enjoy the swaying of the craft on the wide expanses of the Volga. Our plan is to sail as far as Sengilei and take the bus home. The journey should take us three hours. We wake up in Kazan, with our pockets empty and Ivan's shoes gone. Three days later we return home, sailing downriver on rafts, like Huckleberry Finn. The raft people, who ferry logs down from the northern forests to Volga cities, laugh when they hear our story and let us ride for nothing. Ivan entertains them on the way with his jokes and I learn that it is possible to live without a house and to travel without money.

***

My mouth tastes as though a reindeer herd spent the night in it, my head spins and my thoughts crawl away from my grasp. With shaking hands I gather my clothes and tiptoe into the kitchen to dress. I try to smoke the first cigarette of the day without vomiting. I can't go to work without a hair-of-the-dog. A little pile of coins is stacked on the windowsill. I take it and creep out of the house while the others sleep. That night I come home in a happy mood to find Olga waiting for me in a rage.

"That was the last of our money. I put it aside to buy milk for Natasha."

I won't let her see how bad I feel.

"What the hell do you want, Olga? Okay, I drink, but no more than anyone else. You can't say I am a bad husband – I even help you with the washing for Christ's sake – and I don't chase women."

"Just as well. Who'd want a drunk like you?"

"And you don't see me out in the courtyard all day with the domino players. I don't go on fishing trips."

"If it weren't for your leg you'd be off like a shot with your rod and bottles."

I can't bear to be reminded of my leg. I leave for the hostel that night.

There I unburden myself to my friends. "The trouble with Olga is that she thinks she knows better than me because she has a degree. It's a mistake to marry a woman better-educated than yourself."

I get the sympathy I crave from men who are in a similar position to me. I move into the hostel and life becomes a long drinks party, with a little work thrown in for good measure.

***

Olga finds me outside the vodka shop waiting for my hair-of-the-dog. "Vanya, come with me. I've got an invitation to Professor Burenkov's clinic in Chelyabinsk. He's developed a new treatment. It's banned by Moscow so it probably works."

I don't protest as I'm beginning to tire of life in the hostel. Olga takes me home, gives me something to help me sleep, and in the morning we take a train to the Urals.

At the clinic we join 25 other men, each accompanied by his wife or mother. We introduce ourselves. I'm surprised to see the alcoholics aren't all ordinary working men like me. There's a surgeon who confesses he was once so drunk that he fell on top of a patient on the operating table. Next to me sits a Hero of the Soviet Union, with medals on his jacket but no shirt under it. He sold his clothes for a drink. Professor Burenkov says to him: "Well, you defeated the fascists but you allowed vodka to defeat you."

The Hero hangs his head.

Burenkov gives us each a bitter herb drink, then a massive dose of Antabuse. Next we have to down a glass of vodka. The Antabuse reacts badly with the vodka and soon we are vomiting and writhing in pain. It's hard to see two dozen men retch and groan all around you without feeling dreadful yourself. I think I'm going to die. Professor Burenkov strides around the group roaring: "Anyone want another drink?"

The relatives outside are watching the drama through a window. They beat on the glass and cheer: "Give them more vodka!"

Burenkov injects us with camphor and makes us lie on mattresses with our left arms above our heads in order not to strain our hearts. Then he takes us all outside. We sit under trees, feeling life return. The doctor shows us slides of swollen livers and the abnormal brains of the children of alcoholics. That night we take our trains home, clutching our supplies of Antabuse.

As Burenkov's popularity grows throughout the country he stops practising. An unknown number of people die after anxious wives and mothers slip unregulated quantities of Antabuse into food. It has no smell or taste so alcoholics consume it unknowingly and then choke to death after they've had a few drinks. Women usually administer the Antabuse in good faith. They are simply desperate to keep their men folk out of prison.

Before I went to Burenkov it looked as though my days at the factory were numbered. After my cure the administration are so impressed that they put me in charge of the factory's credit fund. This fund is designed to help us buy expensive items such as fridges. It's usually controlled by a group of women supervisors who borrow all they want while telling shop-floor workers that the funds have run out. They say we only want the money to buy vodka. The director dismisses the women and places me in charge. After that every alcoholic in the plant comes to me for three roubles for his troika session.

Now I am sober my thoughts torment me and prevent me from sleeping. To calm me my wife prescribes the popular Hungarian barbiturate Noxiron. At first two or three of these tablets are enough to knock me out but my need soon grows. I drop in on Olga at work and discreetly tear off some blank prescription forms from her pad. I fill them out without trouble as I know the Latin alphabet. As indecipherable as any other doctor's, her signature is easy to forge. Having written several prescriptions I visit different chemists in our area, acquiring enough Noxiron to last a month.

Olga notices that I'm taking a lot of barbiturate and tries to explain that my new addiction is as harmful as the old one. To appease her I stop taking the tablets during the day but at night I swallow them until I pass out.

I share my discovery with my former drinking partners who, like me, have had to choose between alcohol and their wives and jobs. One day when Olga is on night shift my friends come over for a Noxiron session. My wife returns to find me sprawled on the floor, black and blue. When I try to stand up I topple over like a felled tree. I can't even extend my hands to break my fall. The rubbish bin is full of Noxiron packaging. Olga puts me to bed.

That evening a colleague of my wife's and her husband come to supper. I drag myself out of bed to join them. With relief I remember I have some pills left. Excusing myself, I go into the hall and rummage in the pockets of my coat.

"You won't find what you're looking for," Olga stands in the doorway, pointing to the toilet. My hopes of avoiding a horrific withdrawal are dashed.

"Bitch! You had no right to go through my pockets!"

Olga walks away. I follow her into the room, still raging. With one blow I sweep a dish off the table. Jam splatters over our lady guest's new cardigan and the dish smashes the glass of our book-cabinet.

The lady's husband leads me into the kitchen. We smoke and I calm down a little. When we go back into the living-room I find my wife putting Natasha's things into an overnight bag. Everyone leaves.

At the back of a cupboard I discover a bottle of vodka that has been put aside for some family celebration. Although I've been taking Antabuse for several months I open the bottle and begin to drink. I soon pass out.

The doorbell wakes me up. Expecting my wife, I open the door and a policeman enters. "You're under arrest," he saunters through into the living-room, sits down at the table and begins to fill in a form. I go into the kitchen and swallow the remaining vodka in one gulp. After that it is all the same to me whether the policeman takes me off to a health spa or to a leper colony.

4

Prison

"A year! You could sit that out on the shit-bucket!"

My cell-mates in Syzran jail think I've got off lightly for menacing society with malicious hooliganism of a particularly vicious form.

Olga visits me after the trial. "Vanya," she pleads, "I never expected them to send you to prison. I tried to withdraw my statement but they threatened to give me two years for laying false charges. And you heard the judge…"

At the trial she wept and asked them not to punish me, but the judge told her to be quiet.

"Perhaps he was right," I admonish her. "If every wife was allowed to change her mind trials all over the country would collapse and there would be chaos."

We have nothing left to say to each other. If I tell Olga what I think of her she'll walk away believing I deserve to be in prison. "Don't worry about me," I say. "It makes a change to be living here. The company is delightful."

I babble on about prison life until it is time for her to go. She throws me a look of despair as she leaves.

Waiting for the trial was the worst part; now I know how long my sentence will be I settle down to await my transfer to a labour camp. I can't say I am depressed; in fact I'm curious about my fellow inmates and interested to find out what camp life will be like.

In the jail we are housed in long barrack huts that we call cowsheds. As new prisoners come in they talk about what they have done. One or two swear they will never again pick up a knife or a glass of vodka, but most see their arrival in prison as pure bad luck. They don't see any justice in their sentence and are sure it will be their last.

The boy in the bunk next to mine is an exception. Vovik is a country lad of 18 who has been sentenced for robbing village stores. "A thief's life is the best of all," he claims, "I want no other. Robbing those stores is like shooting fish in a barrel: they don't have alarms. We find out beforehand where they keep the money. The assistants leave the takings in the shop overnight because they don't trust their husbands. We helped ourselves a few times and then we went to the Black Sea for a holiday."

"What did you do there?"

"We ate ice cream until we burst and went to the cinema as often as we liked. The trouble was, as we changed the notes we'd stolen our pockets became so weighted down with coins that our trousers hung off our arses. One night in the park we poured all our loose change into a flowerbed. Unfortunately a policeman noticed. He got suspicious and pulled us in. They kicked us round a bit and one of my mates squealed. We each got three years."

"What's the point of stealing a few roubles just to get caught and end up inside like this?" I want to know.

"I never saw ice cream on the collective farm. In Sochi I ate it day and night! Stealing is easy – I'm going to take it up again as soon as they let me out."

Vovik spends his time drawing elaborate ballpoint churches

on handkerchiefs. Prisoners soak these and press them to their backs, leaving delicate tracings which are then tattooed into the skin. Vovik's churches are very popular and he has orders from other cells besides ours. He is a good-natured boy, willing to share out country foodstuffs sent in by grateful village shop-assistants, along with knitted gloves, socks and scarves.

"I'm carrying the can for them," he explains. "They all have their hands in the till too."

I am glad of the odd scrap from Vovik's parcels. I refuse the food my wife sends in but it's hard to exist on prison rations. In the morning we are issued half a loaf of clay-like bread which has to last the whole day. Taking a tip from the old lags, I try not to gobble up my bread at once but keep some to chew in the evening. This is important. Those who eat theirs all at once spend the whole day looking at the others' bread with hungry eyes. Some men develop an insatiable desire for food, begging it from the other zeks. This is the road to losing your human dignity.

I have hardly got used to prison routine in Syzran when the shout comes to pack up our things and assemble outside. We are marched through town to the station. I follow on behind in a cart with four women prisoners. My leg prevents me from keeping up with the men.

At the station we're penned in by snarling Alsatians straining at their chains. With kicks and cuffs the guards make us sit on the floor. Townspeople and travellers mill about but no one stands and gawps. Men casually reach into their pockets as they pass and throw us cigarettes. An old lady pushes past the guards and silently places a bundle of pies on a prisoner's lap.

From the outside, our 'Stolypin' carriages look no different to a normal passenger car except that there are no windows on one side. Each compartment holds about twenty men, and is sectioned off from the corridor by steel bars. Experienced prisoners make straight for the top bunk and kick away anyone who tries to follow them. We have no idea where we're going. Finally, when the train starts to move we learn our destination is to be a camp near Tashkent.

Our bread and herring rations make us crazy with thirst. The guards give out scarcely any water since they can't be bothered to escort us to the toilet. "Have patience lads," says an elderly zek, "salt absorbs water, so if you eat the herring you won't sweat so much. You'll hold water in your bodies and the craving will pass."

As the train pulls into Saratov news comes through that an earthquake has destroyed most of Tashkent. We are diverted to Astrakhan. When we reach that city I am squeezed into a Black Maria with 32 others. A prisoner loses consciousness in the stifling van. No one takes any notice of our cries for help.

The old zek raises his voice: "Okay lads, start rocking."

We lean first to one side of the van and then the other. The vehicle begins to tilt dangerously and the driver stops. The guards unload the sick man and send him to hospital. Then they punish us by taking away our tobacco.

"We once derailed a train this way," says the old man. "When you're looking at 25 years' hard labour you don't care what you do."

***

Corrective Labour Camp No. 4 holds people who have committed crimes against the person. The camp is so near the town that at night we can hear trolleybuses rattling past. While we're waiting to be processed the elderly zek from the Black Maria explains the nature of the camp.

"It's a bitches zone,[17] although there haven't been any here for a long while. However there are a lot of goats.[18] Most of them are SVPs."[19]

Almost half the inmates wear SVP armbands. They help to keep internal order. If for example, an SVP sees someone smoking in an unauthorised place, and the guards are taking no notice, he'll run to the watch and point it out.

Recruitment for the SVP is carried out by the 'Godfather,' the head of the camp. He interviews everyone, explaining that only members of the SVP get remission and other concessions. When my turn comes I decide it best not to tell him what I think of SVPs. Instead I try to convince him of my unsuitability for the role.

"A condition of my sentence is that I am treated for alcoholism."

"We have no such facilities in this camp."

"And I am to serve my full sentence, so what's the point of joining the SVP?"

---

17 Bitches were renegades from the criminal element traditionally known as 'thieves-by-code'.

'Thieves by code' were a criminal caste who refused to work, marry, own property or accumulate money. All stolen goods were pooled. When arrested they would not cooperate with the authorities in any way. From the 1920s onward the Soviet regime set out to destroy this old criminal underworld. Some thieves-by-code gave in under torture and agreed to cooperate with the authorities. They were then known as 'bitches.' In the 1950s special planeloads of these bitches, MVD agents among them, were flown from one camp to another where they fought for control.

If the authorities placed a thief-by-code in a bitches zone he would kill the first person he came across in order to get a transfer. When the death penalty was reintroduced the camp wars quietened down. By the late 1960s thieves-by-code no longer existed except in Georgia. Their successors were known as thieves of the western type, who ran organised crime and illicit business. These criminals formed the Russian mafia and the old type of thief disappeared.

18 Goats were either informers or witnesses for the prosecution.

19 SVPs were an internal camp police force recruited from the prisoners.

The Godfather lets me go.

I didn't become a Pioneer leader in my youth and I'm not about to start telling tales now. Our school teachers wanted to create a nation of stool-pigeons, but fortunately not everyone listened to them. It is the same in camp; the rest of us despise SVPs as the lowest form of human life.

Two SVPs in my cell agree to share all the extra food they receive from parcels and bonuses. When their locker is full one of them hides a razor blade in the other's bed and informs the guard. A search party finds the blade, the culprit gets ten days in the isolator and his friend eats all the food. That incident teaches me a lot about the SVPs' mentality.

Those who work and meet their quotas receive a small amount of money with which to buy goods in the camp shop. Anything unfit for sale in Astrakhan's stores comes to us: piles of stuck-together sweets, dirty sugar, stinking herring and gritty rusks. The shop also sells rough shag tobacco for 6 kopecks a packet. Vodka and tea comes in via civilian workers in the industrial zone. They bribe the guards to look the other way.

On my arrival I go straight to the camp trader and offer my change of underwear for a very low price. Now I can buy enough tobacco to last until my first pay. I won't have to humble myself by begging for it from other prisoners. Another prisoner tells me I'm an idiot, for I could have sold my new pair of pants and a vest for two roubles.

"The idiot was the one who bought them. He paid for rags and I bought independence!"

The next morning new arrivals are assembled for work detail. We are to be sent to an industrial zone to make prefab homes for the virgin lands of Siberia. As we line up one of the camp officers

asks: "Is there anyone here who has completed their secondary education?"

I step forward.

"You will help in the library."

I am lucky to get such a cushy job. In the morning I hand out letters and in the evening prisoners come for books and newspapers. 'Soviet Woman' is especially popular. Pictures of pretty women adorn walls and lockers. The prisoners replace them as soon as the guards tear them down. Convinced that the KGB checks which books they borrow, some zeks take out all 40 volumes of Lenin's collected works.

My days pass easily enough; the only problem is the camp storekeeper, a former colonel, who keeps dropping into the library. This man destroys any lingering respect I might have for epaulettes: only in Russia could such an utterly stupid man have risen to such a high rank. His self-regard is so absolute it shocks me. He shows me the book he is writing. *Life is not a Bed of Roses* describes his life from birth to prison camp. In his childhood he was the top student, he ran the fastest and jumped the highest. In his youth he was more handsome and intelligent than his peers, in the army braver than his comrades-in-arms. His wife was the regimental beauty; he killed her from jealousy.

Our literary journals have already rejected the first volume of the colonel's work; he assumes this is because it contains grammatical errors. Now he wants my help with corrections. I try to excuse myself, saying I'm not very literate, but he persists. In the end I give in. The task oppresses me but I haven't got the courage to tell the colonel the truth.

A fellow prisoner named Oleg comes to my rescue. He is an intelligent lad who dropped out of university. We become friends and spend all our free time together. He helps me proofread the colonel's book and we laugh over it together.

The library is stocked with classics and Dostoevsky's works are constantly borrowed, especially *Crime and Punishment*. But the zeks are only attracted by the title. and return the book disillusioned, having failed to understand its archaic language. I try to warn them in advance: I don't believe that someone of forty can suddenly become converted to Dostoevsky.

I can't work out why the correspondence of our greatest authors should be in such constant demand. I've read Blok's letters and was disappointed – and I'm more educated than most. One prisoner after another borrows Turgenev's letters to Pauline Viardot. Old editions of local papers are also in heavy demand. Finally Oleg explains the mystery.

"Until last year petitioners for divorce had to make an announcement in their local papers. For example: *Citizeness Ivanovna, Anna Semyonova, born 1942, living at 5, Sadovaya Street, has initiated divorce proceedings...*

"Prisoners note down the names and addresses of divorced women and then they copy out Turgenev's letters. Imagine how citizeness Ivanovna feels. She is alone after kicking out the husband who sold all her furniture for drink. Suddenly she receives a letter from an unknown admirer! And written in such effusive language that it makes her head spin. She replies and thus she becomes what we call an external student. Yura and Fedka each have three external students. They sometimes get parcels. There's a woman in our street at home who married a prisoner after she became his external student."

"But can't they see from our address that this is a camp?"

"The zeks say they are working in a secret military plant, which is why the address is just a number. I am sure many women guess the truth but all the same they continue to write. It's better to receive a letter than nothing at all. Remember the joke about two women friends who meet each other in the street? One says: 'How's the old man, drinking?'

'Yes, the parasite.'

'Knocking you around?'

'Yes, the bastard.'

'Well, you can't complain, at least he's in good health.'"

I laugh. Being a married woman in the happiest country in the world is better than being divorced, widowed or single. "Don't you have an external student?" I ask Oleg.

"I don't need one. My own wife's enough. She had me arrested for beating her up. At my trial she pleaded with the judge to let me off but that only annoyed him.

"Lily was the most beautiful girl in town, but everyone despised her because she was born in prison. Her mother came from the Moscow intelligentsia and her father was an army officer, Polish I think. He was shot after the war as a cosmopolitan. After her release from jail Lily's mother got a minus 20[20] so she ended up in Astrakhan.

"Lily's mother was a proud and defiant woman. The locals called her a prostitute. You know what it's like - a single mother coming out of prison, and to make it worse she was a member of the intelligentsia. Lily was a tough kid, always hanging around with the boys and baiting the teachers. She would start a fight for the slightest reason. She often won too, despite her size.

"Soon after they locked me up Lily had our daughter, Sveta. When she wants to see me she comes to the camp, sets Sveta

---

20 This meant she was prohibited from living in the 20 largest cities in the USSR.

down outside the Godfather's office and runs away. Then she phones up and demands my release. Sveta screeches like a stuck pig, the guards can do nothing with her and in the end they give us a special visit. Then Lily takes Sveta away until the next time she decides she wants a visit. If he had the powers the Godfather would probably have released me by now."

The library is separated from the camp schoolroom by a thin partition. School is compulsory for all those under sixty who have not completed the seventh class. Those who refuse have parcels and visits withheld. Teachers are civilian volunteers. The sound of these lessons keeps Oleg and me entertained as we work.

"Masha goes to the shop," the teacher's voice reads out.

Some wit remarks: "It'd be better if she came to see us."

Ignoring him, the teacher's voice continues: "Who can tell me which is the subject of the sentence?"

Silence.

"You, Kuznetsov, come up to the board, please."

"What's the point if I don't know the fucking answer?" grumbles Kuznetsov, but we hear the scrape of his bench.

"Which word is the subject of the sentence?"

After some thought Kuznetsov answers: "Er, Masha?"

"Correct! and which is the verb?"

"Um, 'shop'?"

"No. Anyone else?"

"Of course it is 'goes' but we would say: 'staggers'" another voice pipes up.

"How do you mean 'staggers'?" asks the teacher.

"Well, Masha's obviously got a hangover and is going for a bottle."

"No not, 'staggers' but 'waddles,' because of the huge arse on her."

At that point everyone throws themselves into an impassioned discussion about Masha's qualities and failings, her physique and her temperament.

When exams take place candidates spill out of the classroom into the library looking for us. Together we help them solve problems and correct their written mistakes. The teacher does not try to stop us. The more who pass the better it looks for him.

Our camp has a technical school which is supposed to give inmates skills that will deter them from the path of crime. The yard outside the school is full of farm machinery waiting to be repaired. It is protected from the weather by tarpaulin and guarded by an old man who was sentenced for killing his wife. In her death struggle she hit him so hard with an iron that he has a dent in his cranium the size of a fist. The blow altered his mind.

Oleg and I approach the old man one day. "Look here, Grandad," says Oleg, "it's a pity to sit here all day doing nothing. If you cut this tarpaulin into strips and sew them together you'll be able to make a balloon. We'll bring you some rope; you'll tie your balloon to your chair, and then you'll be able to float out of here. If you leave on a moonless night no one will see you. We won't say anything. It'll be a secret between the three of us."

The old man is excited by the plan and for a whole month he busily sews together pieces of tarpaulin. He is eventually caught, but by this time he has taken to sewing. One day he turns up on evening parade in a marshal's uniform, sewn from tarpaulin bleached white by the sun, and covered in stripes and tin medals made from old fish cans. We cheer as he smartly salutes the camp guards.

It is hard to get used to the camp regime, with endless searches and body counts. For hours we have to stand like sheep in the rain or snow. The semi-literate guards line us up in fives; even so, they usually lose count and have to start again.

Those who want to get out of work cut their wrists or nail their scrotums to their bunks. A man in our cell slashes his wrists with a piece of smuggled razor. I want to call the guards. Oleg just shrugs and says: "Don't be in a hurry; there's not much threat of death when the world looks on."

And it is true; no one dies of a few slashes across their wrists. They do it for show, out of hysteria.

A prisoner named Kuptsev is an exception. He's always hiding somewhere in the basement or under the roof, slitting his wrists and waiting for someone to find him. He never seeks help himself. When I ask him why he does it he replies: "The sensation of blood draining out of my body is like nothing else in the world."

Another man rips his stomach open. He stands smiling at the guards, with his dripping guts cupped in his hands. Stories of people who cut themselves up are usually told with a grin but they're not funny. Everyone responds to cruelty and injustice in their own way.

In camp I find the lack of solitude even harder to bear than the loss of freedom. You're always in a crowd. This is not so bad when you're working during the daytime, but at night you sleep among hundreds of men whose faces you got tired of a long while ago. You start to hate your fellow inmates and they you.

At first I am surprised to see zeks turn on warders for no apparent reason, insulting them and getting punished for it. Then I start to do the same thing myself, just to gain some solitude in the isolator.

In the evenings we exercise by shuffling around a small square. By unspoken agreement the walkers do not disturb each other. If you pace up and down for long enough you start to feel almost light-headed and detached from your surroundings. For a minute or two you can forget you are in a camp. Returning from one of these evening shuffles a tall Jew named Yura Kots approaches me and remarks casually: "Wine drinkers smell different in the morning."

"So they do," I reply, "but what makes you say so?"

"This is going to be the first sentence of the novel that I'll write when I get out of here."

"D'you know the joke about the madman who spent all day writing?"

"Tell me. I could do with a laugh."

"A doctor comes up to him and asks: 'What are you writing?'"

"'A letter,' he replies."

"'Who to?'"

"'Myself.'"

"'And what does it say?'"

"'How should I know? I'll find out when I get it.'"

"But I really am going to write a novel," Kots insists.

"When?"

"When I leave here."

After that Kots and I take our shuffles beside each other. Each month he receives a parcel of books which he passes on to me when he has finished. In the evenings we discuss our readings and study German together.

By profession Kots is a card-sharp, but he was sent to camp for theft. One day he lost to more experienced players. A card debt is a very serious matter. In order to repay it Kots robbed his former college. He was caught trying to make off with a tape recorder and given three years.

I am surprised to see that Kots subscribes to 'Young Communist.'

"What's up, need extra toilet paper?"

"No."

"Then why do you order that rubbish?"

"There are a lot of things written here that you won't find anywhere else."

He shows me some notes on the last page about a debate between Sartre and Camus. This took place a few years ago but everything goes through the USSR like a giraffe's neck and Kots has to keep up-to-date on western literature in order to maintain his pose as an intellectual.

Kots toured the country, presenting himself now as an architect, now as a doctor. He met his victims on long-distance trains or on the beaches of health spas. While he was swindling someone at cards he would remark casually to his victim: "Of course, Camus was not really an existentialist…"

Marcel Proust was Kots' trump card, deadlier than a Kalashnikov in his hands. The credulous intelligentsia, who thought that culture was something you picked up with your university degree, were impressed. Kots would quickly empty his opponents' pockets and then disappear.

Although I admire Kots and envy him his freedom I never think of following his example. A life of crime seems too complicated, and if I'm honest, I know it is beyond my capabilities. Besides, it will inevitably lead me back to prison. I have never held romantic notions about the brotherhood of thieves. They only band together when it is profitable to do so or when they are afraid. It's not hard to give away what has been easily come by, so thieves are accustomed to dividing up their booty. But when it comes down to parting with their last it is a very different story. When they are in difficulties thieves display as much solidarity as spiders in a jar.

No one in my family has been to prison before me. I don't count my father. Those were different times. Besides, that was for a political 'crime.' Nowadays political crimes aren't regarded as crimes at all, although on the outside people still try to keep their distance from former political prisoners, 'to keep away from sin' they say.

Even though I am not attracted to a life of crime I do not condemn my fellow inmates. After two weeks behind barbed wire I learn not to judge others. At first I hold myself a bit aloof. I figure that the other prisoners are probably inside for a reason while I was only put away through a misunderstanding. But I soon realise that most of them are just like me. If you exclude the murderers, bandits and professional thieves, I could stand in the shoes of any one of them. It is only by some happy accident that I haven't been thrown into prison before. I could have been locked up just for all the spirit I stole from work.

And we are not so different from those beyond the barbed wire. Everyone in the Soviet Union steals. Wages are calculated on the expectation that people will do so – if only for their own survival. Collective farmers work for years without seeing any money at all; they would die out like the mammoth if they didn't steal.

This is no accident. Every member of a gang has to dirty his hands with a crime so our government deliberately pushes people towards committing them. If someone then turns round and complains about the system who's going to listen to him if his hands are already dirty?

In fact most prisoners are in jail not for what they have done, but for the time and place of their appearance on this earth. I have to thank God that I was born in 1934 and not 15 years earlier. My wagging tongue would certainly have earned me a bullet in the head during the repression of the 1930s.

I am released in December, after exactly a year. Oleg has to stay inside for another three months. We arrange to keep in touch. His mother and sister meet me at the camp gate and see me off on a flight to Kuibyshev. I don't intend to go back to my wife. I can't forgive her for 365 days and nights behind barbed wire.

5

Opera

"Ahh, Christ just walked barefoot through my heart!" Ivan Shirmanov sighs as he knocks back his first drink of the morning. We are toasting my freedom with a renewed sense of brotherhood.

"Thousands of books have been written about prisons," says Ivan, "but everyone's experience is unique, especially their first. It's been likened to first love, but in the case of love there are doubts: will there be a second? In the case of prison there are no doubts. There will be another and another..."

We finish the bottle and wander down to the market-place, picking up more vodka on the way. There are a few alkashi[21] gathered there. Beaming all over his moonlike face, Ivan offers them a bottle. He watches them drink with an expression as tender as that of a mother spooning porridge into her child's mouth.

Ivan introduces me to one of the group: "This is our Levanevsky who is nothing like his famous namesake.[22] You can always trust him with cash to go and buy a bottle."

---

21 Alkash (plural: alkashi): street-drinker, wino.

22 In the 1930s a Soviet pilot called Levanevsky disappeared while flying over the newly-opened Arctic. His plane was never discovered. It became customary to say 'he's done a Levanevsky' when someone disappeared without trace.

Levanevsky only takes one glass from us.

"Have another?" I offer.

"I don't want any more," he replies. "God is no lovesick swain blinded by his passion. He sees everything. So long as he knows I'm trying he'll give me another chance to sort myself out."

I know that in an hour he'll be shaking like death.

In the market we come across Sedoy the Poet of All Russia. He is standing on an old lady's sunflower seed stall and declaiming to passing shoppers:

> *Through Stavropol, unrecognised,*
> *I wander as a shadow.*
> *And I practise onanism*
> *On International Women's Day!*

"Sedoy was once a teacher," explains Ivan, "a head of department. He was so strict his students nicknamed him Crocodile. Then he took to drink. Now his mother looks after him. Every day you see him in the market in a clean shirt and freshly-pressed trousers.

"There are a lot of alkashi like Sedoy. As former members of the intelligentsia they blame society for their condition. They think it owes them something." Ivan puffs up his chest. "A worker like me would be ashamed to beg or steal; I'll take any portering job I can find."

Amongst the alkashi I meet former teachers, doctors, and engineers. No one respects them for their education; respect is earned by not stealing drinks and not always having your hair-of-the-dog at another's expense. When a person trembles from a hangover it is no great sin to cadge a drink, but the man who does this every morning soon annoys his companions. When alkashi notice that someone is trying to take advantage of them they spit in his face and drive him away. Outcasts can be seen hanging around the fringes of the group, usually sporting black eyes.

Nonetheless, the majority of alkashi try to live at the expense of those around them. 'There are enough fools in this world to be taken advantage of,' is their attitude, and the more people they con the better pleased with themselves they are. Even more degraded are those who see no meaning in life at all. They live from one drink to the next. If you send them for vodka they'll disappear; if you drink with them they'll go through your pockets when you pass out and probably treat you to a bottle over the head as well. One man does this to me and then has the front to come up the next day, look into my eyes and ask: "How come we lost each other yesterday?"

Perhaps he really remembers nothing. Besides, I couldn't swear it was he who hit me. I was too drunk myself to catch him by the hand to look into his face.

***

The pay I collected from camp soon runs out and I have to look for a job. That means sobering up. I know that if I carry on sleeping at Ivan's I'll be led into temptation, so I go to an old friend's flat. Igor Gorbunov comes from the northern Urals where the people speak so fast it's hard to understand them. Like me, he loves reading, but unlike me he is no drunkard, and in the past he has helped Olga extricate me from drinking parties.

Igor has visitors and they are preparing to go camping in the forest. I decline an invitation to join them as I know they'll be taking bottles with them. They set off, leaving me alone in the flat. I sit on the balcony with a book. Across the street is a vodka shop. Troikas are forming at the entrance, pooling their money and sending in one of their number to buy a bottle. It's nearly closing time and sales are speeding up. I need cigarettes so I go down to the shop and join the surging crowd of men around the counter. Elbowing through, I hold out my money amongst the forest of hands.

"Cigarettes!"

"How many?" the assistant asks.

"Two packets."

She frowns at the note I hand her and moves towards the till for change. To save her the journey I involuntarily add: "And three bottles."

I could leave the bottles on the counter but that would look foolish in front of all those people. 'Well, I can always give them to an acquaintance outside,' I reason to myself, but I don't know any of the men who are milling around the shop. So I return to Igor's flat armed to the teeth, put the bottles in his fridge and sit down on the balcony with my book. I try to read but the image of those bottles keeps floating into my mind, breaking my concentration. Almost without thinking, I put the book aside, stand up, go through the living room into the kitchen, and open the fridge door.

The first glassful is hard to swallow. I retch. Holding my breath, I manage to force it down. After a while my throat relaxes and the mouthfuls flutter down like tiny birds. Having seen off the first bottle I feel the need of an audience. I could call on Igor's neighbours but that might be unwelcome, even with two bottles. They hardly know me. Instead I wander down to the yard. I recognise the metal spaceship in the children's play-area.

It has been remodelled from the Decembrist bottle that used to stand at the factory gates. A drunken tune emanates from the spaceship, calling to me like a siren song. Next morning I wake up in the dust without money, documents or shoes.

***

Olga opens the door: "I've been expecting you."

I enter without a word and clean myself up. For a few days we barely speak and I keep out of her way. Finally she can't bear it any longer.

"Vanya, it's my fault you went to prison, but you can't feel sorry for yourself all your life. Make up your mind. Either we divorce, or you put it all behind you."

My resentment boils over. "Thanks to you I was stuck in that hole for a year. Can you imagine the endless searches and body counts, or what it's like to sit down to dinner with a man who's murdered his mother and another who has raped a three-year-old girl? To have the biggest idiot in the province shout at you for no reason when you can't answer back? And you know what the worst thing about camp is? That you're never alone for one minute. Sometimes I felt like committing murder myself.

"You put me through all that and now you want me to behave as though nothing happened. And don't threaten me with divorce. I know you have nowhere to go. You won't humiliate yourself again by going back to your parents."

"All right, I made a mistake, but you can't use that to justify your behaviour forever. You blame me because it gives you an excuse to drink, but in truth you drink because you're a coward. You can't face work, or me, or even poor Natasha. If you can stop blaming me I'm willing to support you until you get paid."

But prison has put an unbridgeable gulf between us. I feel as though I've crossed a boundary beyond which there can be no return to normal life. Olga will never understand what I've been through, and she's mistaken if she thinks I can rebuild a life with her as though nothing has happened.

The factory tells me I can start in the new year. I fill in the time by hanging around with my alkashi friends, who listen to my camp stories with sympathy and even admiration. Their attention fuels my self-pity and I begin to enjoy my role as sufferer. The realisation of this fact does not make me proud of myself, so I submerge myself in drink.

One morning I crawl home to find the flat empty. Olga has taken almost everything that belongs to her and Natasha. I figure she's trying to teach me a lesson and so I refuse to chase her. A week passes. I phone her work. They tell me she's resigned. I'm shocked. They must be lying to me. She has nowhere to go.

Olga left no money so I sell the furniture, including my precious East German bookcase. I haul it downstairs at five in the morning, tie it to Natasha's sledge and drag it to the market. Alas, while I'm taking a smoke-break the wind turns my bookcase over and its beautiful glass doors smash. With great difficulty I convert it into a bottle, which my customer helps me drink.

In the end I sell the only living thing left in the flat, Natasha's hedgehog Yashka. The poor thing is hungry as there is no food in the house. I take it to the shop *Nature*, not really hoping for money. I think that at least someone might take it home for their children, but the shop assistant gives me one rouble and seventeen kopecks for Yashka. She knows the price of a bottle.

Finally I go to my wife's sister Ludmila, who tells me that Olga and Natasha are fine. They're living in a small mining town, they've found a flat and Natasha is going to a modern kindergarten. Ludmila has promised not to disclose their whereabouts. That is the only information I can glean, but I feel calmer. Any decision I take will have to be made with a sober head and so I go home to sleep.

For two days I do not leave the house. Although there is a bottle of vodka in the kitchen I leave it untouched. As each hour passes I feel worse. I can't sleep for a minute. The radio bothers me so I switch it off. I lie down and try to read. A snow-storm howls outside; the wind rattles the window. On the third night I hear breaking glass. 'Bad luck,' I think. Someone must have forgotten to shut their ventilation window and it's blown open and shattered.

The doorbell rings. I go to answer it. On the threshold stands my neighbour Voronin in his underpants. He is holding a gun, a 16 calibre rifle.

"Was it you who broke my window?" he growls.

"What? Are you crazy?"

"Show me your balcony," he demands, and pushes past me into the living-room.

Our balcony is next to his bedroom window. He tries the glass door but it won't open because of the snow piled against it.

"I thought you'd gone out onto your balcony and broken my window with a mop."

"What would I want to do that for?"

"Who the hell knows what goes on in your mind, you've been pissed for two months," he snaps, and goes home.

If I had stepped onto the balcony there would have been footprints in the snow, and there are none. Something isn't right. Why would I break his window? I scarcely know Voronin. He is the head doctor in the clinic where Olga works. We exchange greetings on the stairs and his wife sometimes borrows matches. There's no quarrel between us. After thinking hard about the incident I go to fetch some six-inch nails and a hammer. I nail the balcony door shut. Let them say what they like now! But the business still worries me. And a gun!

The more I think about it the more convinced I am that some sort of dirty trick is being played on me. Voronin knows that I have just come out of camp. He probably knows that Olga has left. He knows that I drink. Perhaps he wants to provoke me into some sort of criminal action. But why? What have I ever done to him? I can find no answer. The simplest solution would be to have a drink and forget it all but I decide not to succumb.

The next day I feel just as bad. It's my third day without drinking. Nor have I eaten anything. I go into the kitchen and listen to the noises in the building around me. Voices come from the landing. I stand by the front door with my ear to the crack but all I can hear is babble, punctuated by whistles and shrieks.

I lie down to read again, but I can't concentrate on my book. The lines dance before my eyes without making sense. I put the book down and lie waiting for nightfall, hoping for sleep to bring relief.

The acrid stench of burning cotton wool annoys me. Earlier in the day I threw my quilt into the stove to warm the room, and now I want to open a window but do not dare after the business with Voronin. I listen to noises outside. The wind has abated and the street roars with cement-mixers driving to the building site down the road.

I hear my name from the other side of the wall. Taking my metal mug, I place it against the door to listen, as I learned in prison. Bloody hell, they are discussing how to get me sent to jail!

"It didn't work last night," says Voronin.

"You must do something to get rid of that parasite." I recognise the voice of a woman who lives on the floor above me. "How can I bring up my children decently with him around?"

"His poor wife," says another, "no wonder she left him. Did you see the low-life he brought in last week?"

'Hypocrites!' I think, 'You bitches aren't averse to the bottle yourselves and when you're drinking the whole block has to know about it.'

I consider jumping out on them but decide this might also be some sort of provocation. If they can accuse me of starting a fight I'll go back to camp for sure.

Judging by the noise everyone in our block is assembled on the landing. Then I hear Voronin address his eldest son: "Dimka, go down into the street and throw stones at the windows. Then there'll be material evidence to have Petrov arrested."

I rejoice. They do not know that I've nailed up the balcony door. But they are many and I am one. I know the disposition of the police well enough. They don't need proof. Once they have their denunciations everything will proceed as smoothly as a knife through butter.

I turn off the light in order to see what's happening in the street. Dimka walks about below, his eyes on the ground.

Hah, he won't find any stones. The snow's too deep.

Dimka begins to gather compressed lumps of snow thrown up by the cement mixers. He throws them at the windows of the block. Fortunately the lumps disintegrate before they reach the third floor.

I shake with fear and outrage. But I'm not going to give up without a fight, so I burst out onto the landing and press the

doorbell of my next-door neighbour. I need a witness to prove
my innocence. My neighbour, a Tatar called Piotr Tukhvatullin,
opens the door, looks into my eyes and silently ushers me into
the kitchen where he pours me a glass of after-shave.

"Drink!" he says, bringing out a chess board and playing with
me for the rest of the night. Sunday morning dawns and Piotr
takes me to the market with him. He spends the whole day
buying animal skins from peasants, keeping me beside him and
giving me a top-up whenever I start to get the jitters. I feel better,
but back in the flat that evening the terror returns. In order not
to hear the Voronins' conversation I go into the kitchen. Apathy
overwhelms me. Let them do to me what they will. Voices start
to come through the wall adjoining the Tukhvatullins flat. Piotr's
wife is cursing him for getting mixed up with me. He defends
himself rather half-heartedly.

I begin to suspect that something is not right at all. I go into
the toilet and pull the chain over and over again. Despite the
noise of the water I can still hear the conversation on the other
side of the wall.

'Delirium tremens! The dt's!' Running into the kitchen I pull
out my emergency supply but it doesn't help. The Voronins have
started to sing. An opera is coming from the other side of the
wall. Voronin is singing solo in a bass voice:

> *From wall to wall with his mug*
> *he runs and listens…*

"He hears nothing!" a chorus of his relations responds.

It is music from *Carmen*. I laugh as tears run down my cheeks.
Why the hell does it have to be opera? I'm an ignoramus where

music is concerned. My only visit to the opera was a reward for washing our bedroom floor in Riga. I block my ears but the voices do not stop. But - if I know I'm hallucinating I haven't completely lost control over myself. I have to do something, so I dress and go outside. It's three in the morning. At the approach of a car I break into a sweat. A dog's bark makes my scalp tingle and tighten in terror, but I press on and manage to reach the first aid post on the main road.

They put me in an ambulance and drive me to the psychiatric hospital at Komsomolsk. Two nurses escort me through the foyer, weaving around male and female patients who are waltzing like somnambulists to the strains of *The Blue Danube*. I laugh till my stomach aches.

I am treated by a Doctor Djmil who convinces me that my visions of the last few days have been nothing more than products of my imagination. Except for the dancers, who were real and part of the Doctor's attempts to give his patients a sense of normality.

I calm down, although I crave a drink. After three days I discharge myself, thinking the best thing to do will be to start work as soon as possible. But my empty flat haunts me with reminders of my family. I run away, seeking out friends who drink.

Two weeks later I return and spend the whole night sweeping up little black devils who have taken over the flat in my absence. There are several hundred of them, about the size of mice, running about the floor thumbing their noses at me and sticking out their tongues. They tease me for imagining my neighbour with a gun. I'm not afraid of them for they seem more mischievous than evil. I take a mop and briskly herd them into the corner so I can crush them all at once. I work as diligently as a woman mopping up spilled water. The task takes all night, for as soon as I have swept the devils into one corner they jump over the mop and run squealing across the floor again.

When my strength gives out I sit down on the bed for a cigarette. The devils run up my trouser legs to my knees, tickling me with their tails. Pulling up my trousers I flick them off onto the floor like cockroaches. But I can bear it no longer and run from the house. I wander all night until my legs bring me back to the hospital. Djmil looks into my eyes and orders me to get undressed. He gives me a massive dose of aminazine and I finally fall asleep.

Half the people in my ward are alcoholic and the rest insane. The alcoholics are treated with Antabuse. However we know that all medicines are poisonous and it is rumoured that Antabuse diminishes potency, so everyone tries to avoid swallowing their tablets. We hide them in our cheeks and then spit them into the toilet.

The first person I meet on the ward is Ivan Shirmanov. A habitual patient in the hospital, he shows me around, telling me not to be scared of the lunatics. Like every supposedly normal person, I am wary of them, but I discover they are not frightening, simply unfortunate. In the course of my life I have met enough people who could pass for psychiatric patients, while some of the hospital's inmates wouldn't be out of place in the corridors of power.

One of the patients has the apt name of Vodkin. He was a chauffeur until drink addled his brain so much he forgot the number of the car he drove. In order not to confuse it with another he would leave the starting handle in when he parked it.

Vodkin's colleagues used to take the starting handle and put it in another vehicle. Vodkin would then spend hours trying to start the wrong car. Eventually he was sacked and sent to hospital.

The nurses take away Vodkin's pyjama bottoms to prevent him getting out of bed, but he manages to pinch someone's dressing-gown and wanders into the smoking-room where the alkies are gathered. His passion is draughts. Despite his imbecility he always wins so no one wants to play with him. To distract him from the board someone asks him to sing, kicking up his heels in a peasant dance Vodkin roars:

> *We spent the night in Samara*
> *With the MVD*
> *They hit us on the neck*
> *We won't tell anybody!*

To encourage him we all join in with the chorus: *The storm raged, the lightning flashed...* until an orderly comes to take Vodkin away and tie him to his bed.

I would do anything to escape the horror of the dt's so in the end I agree to take Antabuse. However, my previous experience has made me sceptical of the treatment. Dr Djmil lends me some books by famous psychiatrists but these only feed my doubts. "Doctor," I tell him, "I have concluded that Antabuse is an unnecessary element in the cure for alcoholism. It works on the basis of fear rather than physiological fact. People who think they're going to die if they drink on top of Antabuse probably will die. It all depends on your state of mind. Antabuse won't work on me any more as I've stopped believing in its effect."

Djmil listens to my argument attentively, frowns and says:

"Vanya, please don't discuss this with the others. Come with me."

He takes me through the wards, pointing at drooling imbeciles.

"That is your future if you continue to drink."

But scare tactics do not work with me.

During my stay at the hospital Djmil tells me about his passion for mountain-climbing. Like many members of the provincial intelligentsia, he understands very well the putrid nature of the society in which we live. He has found a hobby that takes him temporarily beyond the confines of our human world into a battle with the elemental forces of nature. I remember our geography teacher at school and his passion for hiking.

My leg prevents me from hiking or climbing, so I can't follow the path of Djmil and others like him. Other members of the intelligentsia go the way of Sedoy and it looks as though I'm heading in that direction too, not that I consider myself a member of the intelligentsia.

I decide there is nothing more the hospital can do for me, and discharge myself. My first priority is to find Olga and Natasha. Ludmila steadfastly refuses to reveal their whereabouts although I pester her every day. Finally I spot a letter in her box on the ground floor. Pulling it out, I recognise my wife's handwriting. There is no return address on the back but I manage to decipher the postmark: Estonia. I go home and check the atlas – three Estonian towns have 'mining' symbols beside them.

The next morning I haul our washing-machine down to the yard by the rubbish bins and sell it to a passing driver. I buy a ticket to Estonia and set off on the 2,000-kilometre journey, fortifying myself on the way with beer.

After three days I alight from the train at the town of Kivyili,

the nearest of the three mining towns. It is five in the morning.
I take the first bus to the far side of town to begin my search. I
could go to the public health centre but I don't want to embarrass
Olga if she turns out to be working there. After my drunken
journey I look repulsive.

The weather is warm and I go into the park to take off my
sweater. Just inside the gate is a photo display of buildings that
have recently been constructed in the town. One of them is of
a kindergarten built in an unusual style. It might be the one
Natasha attends. After an hour of walking around the town I
find it. It's playtime and I catch sight of Natasha amongst the
children. Making sure she can't see me I wait until the end of the
working day when my wife will come to pick her up.

Olga cannot hide her shock and disgust at the sight of me. "I
suppose I knew you'd find us sooner or later."

I assure Olga that her sister didn't betray her. "All I want is to
have a talk." We buy bread and yoghurt and go into the woods.
Our discussion is fruitless. It's obvious to Olga that I haven't
given up drinking.

"Look, Vanya, let's give it a year. If you can stay on the wagon
for that time we'll come back to you. If not, I'm going to divorce
you."

"Agreed. I'll go back to my parents for a while, get myself
straightened out."

We both know we are kidding each other and ourselves.
Seeing that my journey has been pointless, I find out the time
of the trains and tell Olga not to see me off. I have one rouble
left in my pocket. I buy an ice cream for Natasha and cigarettes
for myself, so that I won't have to be in anyone's debt by cadging
them. It won't be easy to leave Estonia without a ticket so I plan

to hop onto a freight-train. I wait at the station till dusk, when I might be able to slip unnoticed into a goods wagon. However at around ten in the evening my wife appears. She's guessed that I have no money and proposes that I come home to rest in her flat for two or three days until she gets her pay. Taking Natasha she goes to sleep at a friend's house. Before she leaves I ask her to lock the door from the outside.

The dt's begin again that night. While I still have a degree of control over myself I look about for something to distract me. Like any woman, Olga has no tools in the house, but I find a manicure set and use that to take her iron apart and put it together again, over and over again. All night long the neighbours on the other side of the walls sing abominations about me. This time the tune is from *The Marriage of Figaro*:

> *He mends the iron,'*
> *he mends the iron,*
> *he mends the iron,*
> *the irrrrrron... he mends!*

Then the chorus joins in: *Bravo, bravo, bravissimo...*

I find some cotton wool and stuff up my ears but it doesn't help. I run from one room to the other and back again. I take shower after shower, I heat up a large pan of borscht, anything to distract myself from the horrors. Above all I'm afraid of touching the gas cylinder. I imagine that after the explosion everyone will say: "His wife had only just got settled when that drunken bastard turned up and blew the whole block to kingdom come."

In the morning Olga arrives to find me bending over the iron with cotton wool sticking out of my ears. She gives me some medicine that enables me to sleep a little. The following day she sees me off onto the train – no doubt wanting to make sure that I leave.

As we part I reassure her that everything will be all right, but in my heart I know we'll never be able to live together again. Olga can't live with her guilt for sending me to prison and I have no right to inflict my drunkenness on her and Natasha. I can't even bear to see them around me; they are a constant reminder and reproach. Even if I stop drinking I will always feel guilty before them. The only thing to do from now on is get used to living apart.

I am depressed by the thought of losing my daughter. Although I'm of little use to her, she jumped for joy to see her drunken father at the gates of her nursery. And that is no bad thing.

Fifteen minutes into the journey and I'm drinking in the company of three girls who are looking for a fourth to make up a hand at cards. They are already drunk. It would be the grossest indecency to pretend that I don't drink, especially as their invitation coincides with my wishes.

***

Dobrinin pours another glass for my mother. It doesn't take much to make her drunk.

"You can give me all the vodka you want," she shrieks, "but I won't keep quiet. I know you've been with that whore again."

Dobrinin smirks and walks out of the flat, leaving the front door open. He returns with the neighbours from across the landing. They stand in the doorway laughing.

"In case you were wondering what all the noise is about, there you are," he points to my unhappy mother sprawled on the divan. She snarls and tries to fling a book at him but it lands at the foot of the divan.

This is too much for me. I shoo the neighbours out with my stick. Then I turn on Dobrinin and push him against the wall. He sinks to the floor, winded. I go to bed.

"I'll fetch the police. Why did you take that bastard in?" I hear Dobrinin in the next room.

"Shut up. Leave it to me. I'll sort him out."

In the morning my mother looks at me with hatred in her eyes: "What the hell did you attack him for?"

"How can you let him laugh at you like that?"

"It's none of your business. Get out!"

I had moved back to my parents' flat while trying to decide what to do next, Now my decision is made. I move into a hostel and start to drink in earnest with the men who share my room. Others turn up, for we offer warmth and companionship without wives or mothers-in-law threatening to call the police.

I begin work in the DDT factory. My wife's brother is a technician there and he keeps her informed of my condition. Hearing that I'm drinking again she puts pressure on me for alimony, promising to pay it back if I stop. I resent her for trying to control me, even from a distance. In any case I have nothing to send her. My pay-packet comes with the cost of visits to the sobering-up station already deducted. Then I have to pay off my debts. It is impossible to break out of this vicious circle. I cannot afford to rent a room of my own, but to live in the hostel and not drink is beyond human endurance. I try to spend my free time in the local library reading-room, but when I go home I always have to tip someone off my bed.

In the end I decide to leave town. I have an invitation from a former boss, Gantimirov, to go out and work for him at a chemical plant in Chimkent in Kazakhstan. There's nothing to keep me in Chapaevsk. I am tired of that damned hostel, of shop No. 28 and the sobering-up station. I'm sick of my companions, too. They'll forget me soon enough.

I pack a change of clothes and a supply of cigarettes. My younger brother Sashka gives me a tape-recorder and some Vysotsky tapes. Early one morning in the spring of 1968 I leave Chapaevsk on a southbound train.

6

Central Asia

I am awakened by a gentle tap on the shoulder. A policeman stands before me. "It is forbidden to sleep in railway stations, Comrade. Kindly sit up." Giving me a smart salute, he walks off.

Checking my head to see if it has sprouted a crown overnight, I turn to the dosser beside me: "Did you see that? Am I dreaming?"

"Didn't you hear what happened here last year?"

"No."

"Chimkent exploded. It began when the police arrested a lorry driver on his way back from a party. The driver's wife went to fetch his workmates. By the time they reached the station the police had beaten the man to death. They claimed he dropped dead from alcohol poisoning.

"By evening there was no Soviet authority left in Chimkent. The drivers hijacked bulldozers and flattened the police station. Rioters ran through the town killing any cops who got in their way. They sent in troops and in a few days the shops filled with scarce goods. The town calmed down. Then the MVD went round asking questions and people began to disappear. The cops who killed the driver were transferred to another area; their chief became head of a prison camp. You can guess the fate of the rioters who were sent there. Komsomol volunteers and troops kept order in town. We had no police for several months."

I laugh and settle down to sleep again. The next time a cop wakes me I tell him to book me a hotel room; he leaves me alone. A lot of people have moved into the station. At night we gather in the waiting room and listen to Vysotsky; by day we go about our separate business.

I have no luck finding work. Gantimirov is away on a business trip and the plant won't take me on without his approval. I try other factories. There are a lot of jobs going, but none of them provides accommodation. I look for a flat but am offered grim cages so far out of town that I refuse them.

My money is melting like Tien Shan snow, although I'm not drinking and barely eating. In the end I take a train to Tashkent and then jump another to Fergana, where a cousin of my mother's lives. As everyone knows, the tongue leads to Kiev and I find my relative by asking around. He helps me get a job in a chemical factory and the plant gives me a place in a suburban hostel.

The area of Fergana where I live is modelled on the Cheryomushki district of Moscow, with rows of five-storey brick blocks, barren shops and dusty roads. Irrigation ditches run along the streets but these are choked with dead dogs and condoms. Each year new saplings are planted, only to wither and die in the smog of the huge new chemical plants whose chimneys smoke day and night, covering the Fergana valley with filth. In short, the town is not very different to Chapaevsk.

My work is easy enough, but I sweat and chafe in my protective clothing, rubber boots and gas mask. In my free time I hang around the hostel growing bored as there is no TV or other entertainment. I notice the lads who share the hostel never go in to the factory yet they come home in the evenings laden with food and drink.

"Here, Vanya, have some dinner with us," they offer one night.

"No, it's okay, I'm not hungry," I lie.

"Try it, it's dog meat."

"Well, I'll just take some salad." I know people sometimes eat dog meat as a cure for tuberculosis but I don't fancy it. After the lads and I have sealed our acquaintance with a bottle I ask how they managed to live so well.

"We only took a job at the plant to get these rooms and a residence permit. We wouldn't work for the pittance they pay there. Come with us tomorrow and we'll show you how to make some real money."

In the morning we walk down to the railway line. Some men are unloading planks from a goods-wagon, throwing them down as carelessly as if they were shaking matches from a box. Without asking anyone's permission we set about stacking the planks; at one o'clock some Uzbeks arrive to find us leaning against a neat pile. The Uzbeks, who are building a private house, ask us to load the planks onto their cars. When we finish they pay us and treat us to dinner. I earn more for that day's work than I would in a week in the factory.

I come to a decision. From now on I'll give up regular work and become a vagabond. It will be easy enough in Central Asia. If you try to live rough in European Russia you usually end up with a camp bunk as your bed. In Asia you can doss down under any bush and there is plenty of casual work to be found. I'm excited by the prospect of living without the blessings of regular work, the bathhouse on Saturday, and political meetings on Tuesdays.

My new friends and I travel on to Bukhara and Samarkand,

picking up work as we go. I make adobe bricks, dig foundations and paint roofs. We spend our nights at *chaikhanas*, sleeping on low-slung cots that double as tables. In the mornings we drink bowls of green tea as we wait for the wine shops to open. Despite being Muslims, the Uzbeks are fond of alcohol. They also like to sit in circles smoking hashish.

"Try this, genuine Kashgar marijuana!" someone offers me.

It gives me nothing more than a pain in my temples. It's just as well that I don't take to hashish. Being an alcoholic is enough.

In Bukhara I work as a stoker in the brick kilns. You have to be very agile to avoid getting burned. The strongest men make up to 80 roubles a day, an amount which would take me nearly a month to earn back in Chapaevsk. The trouble is that no matter how much anyone earns they never save a kopeck. They drink it all away and I am no exception. I make so much money that I never have to be sober.

After a while the Central Asian climate begins to wear me down. My bones ache and I find it hard to sleep. I decide to return to Chapaevsk. The problem is that however much I earn I can never manage to save enough for a ticket home. After finishing a job I have to toast its completion; by the time I sober up my pockets are empty and I need money for my hair-of-the-dog.

I decide to look for work in a more remote area away from temptation. I return to Fergana, go down to the labour exchange and come to a quick arrangement with a Korean who has a plantation in the mountains. The man takes me up on the back of his motorbike, dipping the machine to left and right around tortuous hairpin bends. On left-hand curves my stiff right leg sticks up higher than my head. My hands are shaking so much from my hangover that I fear at any moment I'll lose my grip and fly off, hurtling down to the valley floor hundreds of metres below. Rising up through clouds that soak our clothes and faces in moisture, we finally reach the plantation. Onions, garlic, watermelons and rice grow on high terraces through which glacier water flows. The Korean's entire family, from tiny children to an ancient grandmother, work from dawn to dusk, yet they need extra labour to help weed the terraces. State investigators are bribed to keep away.

I am given a few roubles a day, food and packets of *Beggars of the Mountain* cigarettes. We work barefoot in freezing water while our bodies are exposed to the burning mountain sun. Our backs blister and our hands crack. At night we drop into pits lined with paper sacks and throw our exhausted bodies onto heaps of old rags.

A cobra slides into our pit. One of the Tadzhik labourers catches it by the neck and prepares to kill it.

"Stop!"

The Korean grandmother peers into the pit. She makes a sign for us to wait. Then she brings a large glass jar with a plastic lid and puts the snake inside. For the next three days she leaves the jar out in the sun. Liquid oozes from the dying snake. We feel sorry for it, but the old lady collects the liquid and uses it to make little cakes. The whole family eats them but we refuse. The Koreans explain that people who eat them will be immune to snakebites for the rest of their lives.

The one advantage of working in the mountains is the absence of alcohol. This enables me to return to Fergana after a month with enough money for a ticket home. Before I can leave town I have to go back to the hostel to pick up my passport. On the way

I notice an inviting bar, with tables laid out under shady trees. I deserve a drink to celebrate, and I'll still have plenty of cash for my ticket.

***

'ALCOHOLICS AND LAYABOUTS!' proclaims our banner in bold white letters on black cloth. We are a filthy procession of swollen-faced men and women. Some have black eyes; some are on crutches. A trolley rolls along behind us, supporting a camera which is filming us for Fergana TV. A local who had a starring role on a previous march tells me that we'll appear on the news tonight.

We parade down the middle of the road in full view of shoppers and passers-by. People laugh and shake their heads but no one shouts abuse. They probably think: 'There but for the grace of God go I.'

The police picked me up after finding me passed out in a ditch. They hosed me down, put me in a cell for the night and in the morning forced me to stand in the yard with the other detainees while the superintendent lectured us on the evils of drink.

When we return from the penitential march they make us pay for our night's lodging and fine us each 25 roubles, except the two men who carried the banner. They're excused five roubles of their fines, which no one begrudges.

After my release I go back to the labour exchange. I am hired by another Korean with a plantation in the mountains, but again on my return I drink away my pay before I can reach the railway station. It's the same story all summer. I take jobs in Kuvasai and Kizil Kiya in Kyrgyzia. Finally, when the weeding season ends, I manage to reach the railway station without being diverted and settle down in the station buffet to wait for the Tashkent train. My disreputable appearance must have given me away: a cop comes over and hauls me off. Fortunately some foreigners are staying in Fergana so I don't have to repeat the penitential march.

The police want to know why I haven't paid my first fine. I'm still registered at the chemical plant so I say I'm waiting for my wages. The superintendent tells a policeman to escort me to my hostel to collect my passport, which they will hold until I pay off my fines. The policeman and I set off on foot. The man is so tired after his night shift that he lets me continue alone, making me promise to hand in my passport the next day. That's the last the Fergana police see of me. I pick up my passport and head for Margilan.

At Margilan station an Uzbek buys me a ticket and in return I smuggle a caseload of tomatoes to Tashkent for him. I find that city in uproar after a spontaneous explosion of nationalism during a football match between the local Milk-Churners team and the visiting Ukrainian Miners. Rioting spreads into the streets after the game. The police and local militia are busy breaking up fights and beating up anyone they can find. Train passengers are warned not to walk into the town. I spend a few days in the station trying to find a way home. The conductors on Moscow-bound trains are unusually strict and won't let me on without a ticket. At last a Kuibyshev train pulls in. I approach a young conductor standing on the platform.

"Hey mate, take me along with you."

He looks me up and down: "Have you got any money?"

"Not a kopeck. If I had I would've bought a ticket."

The lad laughs and asks sarcastically: "Would a ride as far as Kuibyshev suit you?"

"It would. Then I can catch a local train."

"So three thousand kilometres isn't far enough for you! Where is your final destination?"

"Chapaevsk," I reply, looking around to see if I might try my luck elsewhere.

"You're from Chapaevsk then?"

"Yes."

"What part?"

"Bersol."

"You're kidding!"

"What's the point of lying? The train's about to leave and we'll never see each other again."

"Wait," he says, "what street do you live on?"

"Clinic street."

"Do you know anyone on Short Street?"

"Lyokha Pop"

"What about Lyuska Trepalina?"

"Everyone knows her."

Lyuska is the local whore. She hangs around the hostel where I lived. I've only spoken to her a couple of times but that's enough for the conductor to let me on board.

The train departs and I settle down in a window-seat. The endless steppe slides past, as smooth as bone, broken only by a dry shoreline that was once lapped by the Aral Sea. When we stop at desolate towns the conductor, whose name is Yura, does a roaring trade selling vodka and cigarettes to crowds on the platform.

"There's no alcohol or tobacco in their shops," he explains. "I have to give a cut to the station-master and chief conductor but I make enough. Have a drink."

***

My friend Oleg from the Astrakhan camp asks me to come and stay with him. I sell some blood to help the Vietnamese victims of American aggression and buy a ticket on the steamer *Sergei Uritskii,* an old man of the Volga built in 1912. It stinks of dried Caspian roach and the over-ripe melons that are piled high in baskets on the upper deck blocking everyone's way. It is pleasant to sit on the passenger deck in old wicker chairs under a canvas canopy. Cream silk curtains flap like sails through open windows. For two days and nights I gaze at the shoreline, mesmerised by the gleam of distant cities and hydro-electric power projects.

In Astrakhan I find Oleg living in a district built in the popular Cheryomushki style. Although he has an official job checking shop burglar alarms he earns his money in billiard halls. We settle into a routine. I take over his rounds while he goes off to play. After lunch I join him.

Pretending not to know Oleg, I bet on the outcome of the game. With a prearranged signal he lets me know how it will end. That way we always win. If he loses I collect money for backing his opponent; if he wins our takings are doubled. No one knows me in the town and we do not broadcast our friendship. All the same we don't win much, just enough to feed ourselves and the family.

Oleg is on the wagon which is fortunate as drinking and billiards do not go together. Fights in billiard halls are common and so is cheating. When an apparently stronger player loses there's always a post mortem which rarely ends peacefully. The winner often has to beat the money out of the loser. It is forbidden to play for money so Oleg and I have to be careful. If caught making bets we'd go straight back to prison.

Life would be fine apart from problems on the domestic front. Oleg and his wife Lily fight day and night. Their punches, slaps and screams end in no less violent reconciliations. The police have long since stopped responding to neighbours' complaints. They know that by the time they arrive the combatants will be locked in such a tight embrace it will be impossible to prize them apart. If they manage to arrest Oleg then Lily will turn on them like a tigress. Once when they try to arrest her, Oleg dangles their daughter out of the window until the police let her go.

It is impossible to live in this atmosphere so after a month I decide to return to Chapaevsk. Before I leave, Oleg takes me to a village near the sea where we buy 1,000 dried bream for a fantastically low price. In Kuibyshev these fish are in great demand as an accompaniment to beer. I can sell them for enough money to support me for several months.

As luck would have it the *Sergei Uritskii* is waiting in dock. I manage to buy a ticket for a place on deck and board just at the last minute. As I am arranging my bags I hear a familiar voice.

"Vanya! Going back already? Didn't you find your friend?"

It's one of the waitresses, Asya, who I got to know on the journey down. "I did," I reply, "but a husband and wife make one devil. I felt uncomfortable in the middle of their quarrels. I'm going home now to sell my fish."

"But you have so many bags and no berth."

I smile: "I'm alright. I'll sleep under the stars again."

Shyly Asya asks me to share her berth.

As the ship approaches Kuibyshev I ask for her address. She shakes her head. "It's better not to raise hopes. They are too easily crushed."

Asya is one of those rare women who are untouched by the

filth of this world. I could have arrived home not only without the bream but without trousers, money or documents. Robbing me would have been as easy for Asya as spitting.

Back in Chapaevsk I decide not to sell my fish to the thieves and swindlers who run the market. Instead I give them to my uncle Volodya in return for an advance. By the end of the week I'm back on the bottle again and have forgotten all about the bream. As luck would have it I bump into Yura the conductor and am able to thank him properly for the ride.

I move into another hostel. It is built like pre-war barrack housing except it's made of brick and has an indoor toilet. All day long snotty children play in the corridor under lines of grey underwear. Everyone knows which pair of underpants belongs to whom. If a brassiere falls on the floor you can pick it up, examine it and identify its owner by the way it is patched. Then you knock on her door: "Auntie Dusya, here's your bra. The kids were using it as a football."

Domestic rows blow up with boring regularity. Every family drinks. The noise only abates in the early morning when the bottles are empty and the shops still shut.

Each morning my hangover gets me out of bed, just as if I was going to work. I gather together bottles from the night before and go next door to shop No. 28 to exchange the empties for a glass of cheap fortified wine. This disgusting brew helps me control myself until ten o'clock when the spirits section opens.

In the morning my hands shake so much that I can't hold a glass without spilling it over myself. If I have a companion with me he pours the wine down my throat; if not I use a belt. I wrap one end round the hand that holds the glass and pass the other around my neck, pulling on it until the glass reaches my lips.

On the days when the shop is out of wine we have to look for eau de Cologne or aftershave lotion. These are hard to drink on an empty stomach. Furniture polish is the worst – that is real poison and always makes me puke. However, once I've lined my stomach with a hair-of-the-dog I can drink whatever comes my way.

Alkies from the whole district congregate in my room. It's warmer than the street. I open the day's session by banging my fist on the table:

"What's the fucking use of thinking?

Fill your glasses and start drinking!"

Each person takes a bite from a stale hunk of bread on the table as they pass the bottle around. If a new face appears at the door I shout: "Come in! Welcome to the communist state. Don't worry about a thing. Put on what you like and sleep with who you like. In the morning we sort out clothes and girls."

I try to avoid my former workmates. They are all drinkers too, but unlike me, they don't comb the shops for lacquer and varnish. Occasionally I see my mother in the streets and then I have to duck out of her sight. Unfortunately ours is a small town, and local gossips inform her of my descent into street drinking. When she comes down to shop No. 28 and bundles me into a taxi I resign myself to the inevitable. My mother has a bag already packed. We drive out to a hospital at Rubezhnoye, a former country estate where Catherine the Great's lover, Count Orlov, kept thoroughbred horses. After the revolution the house was converted into a hospital, but 50 years of Soviet power have brought it to a state of collapse.

The director turns a blind eye if patients get drunk on occasion; the most important thing is to repair the place. A condition of treatment is that each patient has to work four hours a day without pay. They paint and plaster walls and build the director's dacha in the grounds. My job is to watch the hospital's water tank, making sure it never overflows or runs dry.

"Go on, drink your damned vodka! Drink the filthy stuff!" the doctor stands in the middle of our circle, conducting us like a circus ringmaster. We each have a bucket between our knees. The doctor has injected us with apomorphine before making us swallow a warm solution of bicarbonate of soda. Then we drink vodka from the three bottles we have each been told to bring with us to the hospital.

The doctor examines everyone's bucket. I can't manage to throw up, so he makes me drink a mixture of vitriol, castor oil and grease. The next morning I stick two fingers down my throat while the doctor's back is turned. Anything is better than drinking that dreaded cocktail again. After a dozen sessions I start to vomit blood and they take me off the treatment – a blood vessel has burst in my stomach.

Next we're treated with Antabuse, with a cruelty and intensity I have never yet experienced. After my dose the doctor makes me drink 20 grams of vodka. I suffocate. My chest feels as though it's being crushed by rocks. As I struggle for breath the doctor holds up a hand mirror. My face turns purple and then deathly white. My hands and feet are freezing. The doctor gives me oxygen, wraps me in blankets and monitors my blood pressure.

With each treatment they increase the dosage of vodka. When I return to consciousness, only half alive, the doctor leans over me and says: "There, you see, in hospital, in the presence of a doctor, you almost died. What will happen to you if you have a drink outside? You will die! You'll die gasping like a dog!"

Despite this torture I still do not believe in the efficacy of

Antabuse; however I stay off the bottle for a few weeks after my release. I hope to keep sober for long enough to find a more interesting circle of friends. I am sick of hanging around the vodka shop with completely degraded people. After my two unsuccessful attempts to escape Chapaevsk I begin to suspect that I will only find the company I desire in Moscow. In the capital there must be people who live life in the fullest sense of the word, who write novels and read poems to each other. But how could I live among those parasites? They think they are above us provincials, all the while bleeding us dry, living off our backs. They think themselves so superior, yet to boast that you are a Muscovite born and bred is as absurd as boasting that you were born on Saturday.

Even if I decide to go to the capital I'll have to live rough as I know no one there. And all those plate glass windows reflecting the ugly curve of my leg will be a constant reminder of my disability.

Instead of Moscow I go out to the steppe. My sister's husband Yura keeps bees and he needs someone to watch the hives during the summer.

The last remnants of the ancient forest that once covered most of Kuibyshev province were cut down during the Great Patriotic War.[23] Now the steppe-land crops are protected from dry winds by strips of plantation. These trees have grown from the saplings which my classmates and I helped to plant twenty five years ago.

Along the edge of the plantation are some 80 beehives belonging to different owners. They take it in turns to bring me food, water, tea and cigarettes. Yura lends me a tent, a camp-bed and a pair of Wellington boots. He offers me a dog but I don't want one. She'll bark at every wild animal that passes.

---

23 The Great Patriotic War is the Russian name for the Second World War.

I quickly become attuned to the life of the forest. After a few days I put my watch away; I've learned to tell the time by the sun and the stars. I notice that the magpie chatters in quick alarm at the approach of a human, while his chatter has a different timbre when an animal approaches. When the ants begin to scurry, trying to cover the entrance to their nests, I know it's time to take some dry wood into my tent. Sure enough, leaves rustle, the mosquitoes bite more viciously, and I hear the first patter of raindrops on my tent roof.

The birds will not let me sleep through the forest dawn, but that is a blessing. I rise to the nightingale's song, edging out of my tent and sitting absolutely still, not even smoking. The bird takes no notice of me and sings on, beautifully and forcefully. It is not just singing for love, for the female is already sitting on her eggs. I wonder where that power comes from.

When the nightingale falls silent I set off to look for mushrooms. In my childhood Grandfather Dobrinin taught me how to search for them; he even knew by the smell of the wood what type of mushrooms grew there. The best time to look for them is after rain. I gather two basketsful of saffron milk-caps, orange-cap boletus, russula and agarics. By some oaks I strike it lucky and find the prized honey agaric. I give most of my mushrooms away to the beekeepers when they arrive with my provisions.

The next day I go to the steppe to pick bunches of St John's wort, greater celandine and milfoil for my sister who uses them for folk remedies.

Rainy days get me down. It's boring and uncomfortable to sit in the tent for hours on end. I ask Yura and the others not to bring vodka but all the same I feel restless. To distract myself from my thoughts I carve pieces of wood into statuettes and decorate bottles with plastic telephone wires. I learned the technique in prison. With a hook made from a bicycle spoke I twist the plastic into pictures and designs. When I've finished I give the bottles to the beekeepers who are happy to take them home to their wives.

The mosquitoes annoy me, but I know from my experience in the taiga that the only way to defeat them is to take no notice. I have no net; I don't want to shut myself off from the world around me. Just before rain, when the midges and mosquitoes become a real torment, I drive them away with the help of a beekeeper's smoker. It is a simple can with holes punched in it and attached to a string. Inside I put some rotten wood and a piece of amadou fungus pulled from an old tree stump. When struck with a flint the amadou smoulders and lights the wood. Smoke billows from the can as I swing it like a church censer.

Just as I used never to tire of looking at the sea, so I sit for hours gazing across the blue undulations of the steppe. Sometimes a rare bustard hovers overhead, or a distant herd of boars runs through one of the gullies that scar the landscape. Seven centuries ago Mongol horsemen, not knowing how to live in the forest, camped on these grasslands. A lorry raises dust on a far-off road. I half close my eyes and imagine I see horsemen of the Golden Horde galloping along the crest of a ridge.

Summer ends. I pack up my tent with sadness. Yura drives me back into town. Each beekeeper gives me a kilo of honey and a small sum of money. I have nowhere to go except the hostel. My former plant will not take me back because of my poor work record. I curse them all to hell and exchange my honey for samogon.

7

Labour camp

There is nothing but Benedictine on the shelf of shop No. 28.

"Let's buy a bottle," I suggest.

My mate Tarzan explodes: "Are you crazy? That's a women's drink. Let's get some cucumber face lotion from Auntie Dusya."

"But Benedictine's stronger than vodka. I used to drink it in Riga."

"Okay, you win."

Tarzan and I wander off to the park with our Benedictine. We are on our third bottle when Pashka Plaksin joins us. Pashka is famous in Chapaevsk as an alcoholic and a master-sewer of felt boots. As there is no chance of buying good boots in the shops, many people make them on the quiet. Pashka's boots are the best in town. To own a pair is like having a Pierre Cardin suit in your wardrobe. Those who want to jump the queue will slip him a bottle of something. This is how Pashka became a drunkard. In the mornings he shakes so much he can't even pull up a glass with his scarf. Someone has to slip a stick between his lips and pour the wine straight down his throat.

Pashka produces two bottles of pure surgical spirit donated by a grateful customer. The next thing I know is an agonising pain in my head and back. I open my eyes to see someone giving me an injection.

"What did you drink?" a voice asks.

"Surgical spirit," I rasp.

"You can't get that in the chemists. Where did it come from?"

"A friend gave it to me."

"That was no friend. If the police hadn't found you and brought you here you would have died. That was industrial spirit and it has burned up your kidneys."

It seems that after leaving Tarzan and Pashka I fell into a snowdrift. Some passing police pulled me out and hauled me in to the sobering-up station. A nurse declared me to be on the point of death so they called an ambulance. It would have spoiled their records if yet another drunk died in their charge.

The hospital washes out my kidneys and discharges me. Sober again, I am taken on by a plastics factory. Now I remember how much I hate the working life. When I was drinking the only problem I faced was how to get over my hangovers; now I'm working like a donkey for nothing in return. I hardly earn enough to buy bread. Most of my pay goes to the sobering-up station which I have visited 14 times since returning from the forest. Soon I stop going to work; it seems futile.

The local police are sick of the sight of me. The next time they pick me up they give me a beating and put me on a charge of drunken hooliganism. They wait five days for my black eyes to fade, but even then the judge at my trial asks: "What happened to your face?"

"A bag of fists fell on my head."

The judge decides I am capable of responding to treatment and sentences me to two years in an LTP.[24] It lies about thirty miles

_____

24 A punitive treatment centre: basically a labour camp for alcoholics who were also supposed to receive treatment.

away, beside the village of Spiridonovka. Life in the LTP is easier than in other camps for we are classed as sick men rather than criminals. Our guards are unarmed and letters are not censored.

The village of Spiridonovka is a miserable collection of hovels surrounded by a strict-regime camp and the LTP. While the village children play 'prisoners and warders,' driving each other in convoys through the mud, their parents work in the camps. The villagers dedicate themselves to taking care of the prisoners, smuggling in vodka, cigarettes and an astronomical amount of tea.

Treatment is compulsory but I categorically refuse to take Antabuse, despite a promise of time off my sentence if I do so. In the past I've swallowed it voluntarily; I won't have it forced down my throat. They send me to the isolator a few times then give up on me.

The doctor in charge of our treatment is a sadist called Bityutskaya. "You will not receive parcels here. You've already caused enough suffering to your families," she announces. This doesn't make much difference to me as I have no one to visit me or send in food. Later many of us paint '*In Vino Veritas*' on the back of our jackets. When the doctor walks past we turn our backs so she can fully appreciate the effects of her treatment.

As I walk into the barracks with the other newcomers an older man comes up and introduces himself: "I'm Vassya-the-thief-alias-Honeycake. I've been through Rome and the Crimea, fire and water, brass trumpets and devil's teeth. I'm the orderly around here, so any of you who fancies a cushy job has to clear it with me first, okay?"

Vassya gives us the once over. Spotting a defeated-looking country lad, he asks: "You there, what's your name?"

"Trofim Ivanich."

"You look like an intelligent chap, Trofim. Give me a goose and you can guard the stationery store."

Trofim persuades his wife to smuggle in a goose. She probably feels guilty for having committed him to the LTP. Trofim is delighted to be given such an easy job and goes off to perform it conscientiously.

At evening roll-call there's one person missing. Ten recounts establish that the absent man is Trofim.

"Where the hell is he?" asks the guard.

"Working," someone remembers.

"Where?"

"Guarding the shop," replies an innocent newcomer.

"Who told him to do that?"

"One of the orderlies," replies another innocent.

No one can prove anything against Vassya; the goose has already been eaten. Trofim has received his first lesson in camp life.

Unlike many inmates, Vassya is fond of talking about his past: "I grew up on a farm in the Kuban. When the Nazis arrived in '42 I went to work for them as a groom." He pauses. "Don't turn up your noses, brothers. I had to eat. They needed me to look after their horses so they took me with them when they retreated. We ended up in Hungary. By then it was obvious to any idiot that the Germans were losing the war. I slipped away and joined up with our boys in Poland.

"After the war I went home to the Kuban and everything would've been fine if my mother hadn't had to show off to the women at the well. Her neighbours were boasting of their sons' exploits so she produced a picture of me with my chest covered

in medals. Someone noticed these were fascist decorations. I had
borrowed a regimental dress for the photograph; I could hardly
pose with a broom and bucket of horse shit. So I was denounced
and given ten years for collaboration.

"Since then I've been in more camps than I can count. The
truth is I don't care much for life on the outside, what with
residence permits, housing queues and trade union meetings.
After a month I'm ready to see the inside of barbed wire again."

Early one morning a huge turd appears in the snow near the
accounts office where officers' wives work. It is about twelve
centimetres in diameter. Beside it lies crumpled newspaper and
a pile of dog-ends. A group gathers around the monstrosity. It
could only have been produced by a giant – yet normal-sized
footsteps lead to the spot.

Vassya appears to be more affronted than anyone else. "Citizen
lieutenant," he says to the officer who has come to inspect the
offending object. "This is disgraceful hooliganism, especially
in the presence of women. I propose that everyone's orifice be
measured in order to find out who is capable of such an outrage."

I have my own suspicions, for that week I noticed Vassya
collecting something in a plastic bag which he kept carefully
hidden away. After the fuss dies down he confesses his deed to
a group of confidants. He says he learned the trick in a camp at
Komi.

In the work zone we make shell-timers for a Kuibyshev arms
plant. Many zeks throw themselves into the job as a distraction
from deadly boredom, but none of them gets remission. The
only guarantee of early release is membership of the SVP. Some
zeks think: 'Okay I'll put on the armband but I won't inform on
anyone.' But it doesn't work like that: a zek betrays his fellow

inmates as soon as he dons that armband. In a day or two he is racing the other SVPs to the guardhouse to sing for a two-rouble bonus. Weakness of character turns people into informers, and once they have crossed that line there's no turning back.

We are a friendly brigade. When someone nears his release date we give him a hand so that he can save some extra money. Although the work isn't too heavy we depend on chefir[25] to meet our targets. Tea is smuggled in by civilian workers and by the prisoner who goes to the village post office for our mail. Zlodian Kitten is the only prisoner allowed out without a guard. He is an artist who paints pictures of kittens on glass to sell in the village. His kittens are all different, with bows and balls and so on. As the local shop only sells portraits of Lenin, there's a huge demand for his work. Zlodian never returns without loose tea slipped in between the pages of newspapers.

After I've been in Spiridonovka for a year the authorities finally realise that the fight against chefirists is not only useless but counterproductive. A prisoner high on chefir works like a robot. No tea means no target, so the rule is relaxed and production plans are filled.

My co-chefirist is a drug addict known as VV. More of a dabbler than a hardened addict, VV takes any tablet he can lay his hands on. He is particularly fond of teophedrin, a mixture of codeine and ephedrine.

"I was a good Komsomolist before I did my military service, but the army changed that. It wasn't so much the bullying that got me down, though that was bad enough. No, it was being surrounded by so many idiots who felt important for the first time in their lives. Now I spit on everything.

25 Chefir was extremely strong tea.

"It was my mother who sent me here. She didn't like the company I fell into after I left the army. It wasn't what she had in mind for her only son."

VV and I share our tobacco and vodka, most of which comes into the camp in hot-water bottles thrown over the fence. Almost everyone who is freed from the LTP remembers his mates this way.

I grow tired of dormitory conversations about who drank how much and who slept with whom. To relieve the boredom I devise a joke. I write a letter purporting to be from 'Sima,' the wife of 'Fedya.' When letters are given out all the Fyodors in the barrack come forward but none recognises the handwriting. There is no return address on the envelope. Then by collective decision the letter is opened and read aloud. It could have been written to any one of us: *Divisional Inspector Paramon often drops by…* this was interrupted by a roar of knowing laughter… *At last I have dried out the mattress…* the reader continues as 300 voices jeer at the unknown Fedya for wetting his bed… *I salted the cucumbers and yesterday in the herring queue Paramon's wife Agafya slapped my face…*

In the morning all the Fedyas in the camp come forward to prove their wives are not called Sima. One of them, who happens to be married to a Serafima, brings a collection of letters to show that her handwriting is not that of 'Sima.' A week later another letter arrives from Sima. The contents reveal that she has had a reply from her Fedya. The whole zone sets out to uncover the mysterious man. Only after a third or fourth letter do people start to guess that I am the author. They clamour for more: "We want something to cheer us up after work."

A wave of prison riots breaks out all over the country.

Discontent also grows in our camp. A new Godfather arrives and begins a campaign of intimidation. Our letters are torn open before they reach us and visitors are roughly searched, especially women. When a prisoner from the neighbouring criminal zone goes on the run they start to torment us with endless counts and recounts. A guard marches through our barrack with a slavering Alsatian on a slackened chain. It lunges at us; a couple of men who protest are taken out to the punishment cells.

They say you can divide people into cat lovers and dog lovers, but I'd add a third category: Alsatian lovers.

That night we gather to discuss what to do. Someone suggests writing a letter to Brezhnev, another says we should kill a dog. Suddenly, unexpectedly even to myself, I leap onto a bunk and shout at them: "Tossers! Cowards! All this talk is useless!"

The protestors turn to me, some try to knock me off the bunk. Others ask: "Well, what do you suggest then?"

"A strike! We stay in bed tomorrow and refuse to go to work until our demands are read by higher authorities. We'll write a list of complaints and smuggle a copy out to the newspapers. If the authorities refuse to give way we'll go on hunger strike."

"Idealist!" mutters an older prisoner, but most of the men agree to my proposal. We choose a committee of four volunteers and I write out a list of complaints.

The next morning no one leaves their bunks except the cook and the man who stokes the boiler. Not everyone is happy to strike, especially those nearing the end of their sentences, but they don't want to oppose the collective will. The Godfather arrives, stomping through the barrack, at first abusing us and then trying persuasion. Four men hand him our list of demands and he goes off to phone his superiors.

A week passes and then an MVD commission arrives. To our amazement, half our demands are met. Weapons are removed from the zone, we are allowed to wear sweaters and warm underwear, the food improves, visitors' rooms are enlarged, they promise to put a TV in the rec. room. and to supply any books we request. I immediately compile a list and they bring in all the books I have ordered, even ones that are forbidden on the outside such as Schiller-Mikhailov's *History of the Anabaptists.* I expect they can afford to be generous because their libraries are overflowing with confiscated books.

Despite these concessions the Godfather continues to censor our letters. My friends and I start to write to ourselves, posting letters via different channels. We cover the pages with meaningless words, sprinkled with numbers and symbols. Let him waste his time trying to decipher these, we laugh.

Thanks to the barrack stoolies, the Godfather knows the strike was my idea. He has his revenge when VV and I get completely pissed at work. One of our freed companions has thrown a bottle over the fence. Medvedev, the officer in charge of our work brigade, drives us back to the barracks saying we'll face the music in the morning. When he tries to follow us into the barracks we rush at him, flapping our arms and puffing vodka breath in his face. "Phoo, phoo, phoo, get out, get out."

Medvedev has not brought an escort, so he leaves, muttering threats. A few minutes later guards come and haul us off to the isolator.

In the morning Medvedev rages at us: "You'll be punished under article 77 for interfering with an officer in the line of his duty and causing mass disorder."

This charge is considered worse than murder and punishable

by anything from eight years to execution by firing squad. We refuse to answer questions or admit to anything. "Bring the Godfather. We won't say anything until he's present."

Medvedev laughs in our faces. "I can assure you that he will not come."

"But he must. He is head of the camp."

"He won't."

On hearing this we begin a hunger strike. A few days later a Black Maria takes us to Kuibyshev jail. We learn that our strike was in vain, because the Godfather was away on holiday that week.

Kuibyshev jail is full of men who have taken part in a riot that makes ours look like a children's tea party. I hear about it from a prisoner in my cell: "It began when a packet of tea was thrown in. It landed on the strip of ploughed earth between the inner and outer wires. As a prisoner stretched his hand through to recover the tea a guard shot him in the leg. News spread around the zone. When the SVPs got wind of a revolt they ran off to the guard house. A couple of them who didn't make it were beaten to death.

"We broke into a workshop and found a tank of diesel fuel. We soaked our jackets in the oil, lit them and threw them through the windows of the guards barracks. That set the zone on fire. Some prisoners armed themselves with iron bars and took over the isolators, killing a guard in the process. That day we were possessed by a sort of demonic joy.

"The camp director tried to stop us. I have to admit he was a brave man, for he came out without an escort. He seemed to be prepared to listen so we started to tell him our grievances. Then a zek lost his patience and hurled a waste bin at the director's head. Rage took over again and the director was severely beaten. He died later.

"No one touched the nurses in the camp hospital. One of the zeks with authority led them across to the guard room. The cruel thing is, I've just heard he got eight years. They said that if he had the authority to protect the women he might have intervened to end the riot.

"Troop carriers surrounded the zone and a helicopter circled overhead. A voice shouted over loudspeakers: 'Citizen prisoners! Cease this mass disorder immediately!' We began to wonder why the soldiers didn't storm the place to restore order. It seems they were waiting for orders from Moscow.

"When the day ended we realised we had nowhere to sleep and nothing to eat. We threw stones at anyone who tried to enter the zone, but the night was cold and by the next morning we'd lost our enthusiasm. They came for us in Black Marias and we no longer had the energy to defend ourselves.

"We were sent to different jails. They took me to Syzran, where I opened my big mouth. Some bastard of an SVP overheard me and here I am, looking at another five years. I didn't even kill anyone or beat the guards. What a mess. If I hadn't got mixed up in that business I'd have been out next year."

This man's story depresses me, for I too am looking at a longer sentence, and this time it will be in a camp rather than a 'treatment centre.'

***

Fortunately for us, Medvedev can't produce a witness at our trial. When we threw him out of the barrack there was only one other man present and he was in a state of Antabuse-induced psychosis, cowering in a corner pointing a piece of plywood at

Medvedev and shouting: "Bang! Bang!" Our charge is reduced to hooliganism. Even so, we get four years each.

Four years! I torment myself imagining this endless length of time. But my cellmates congratulate me. Well done! That's nothing! It's true that many people get longer sentences for lesser crimes but I fear I'll go out of my mind.

Then the impossible happens. Our sentences are overturned thanks to VV's mother. As director of a Syzran department store, she is an important person and able to hire a good lawyer who wins our case at the court of appeal. The judge simply orders us to serve out the rest of our original sentences – a year in my case – in a different prison. VV and I are moved to Barkovka near Toliatti.

The camp at Barkovka is strict regime, full of SVPs and headed by a bastard called Dubov. It lies near an industrial dump which burns continually, shrouding the area in black smog.

The industrial zone is a brick-making plant separated from the living area by a high fence with gates and watch-towers. The factory works around the clock, one brigade taking the heavy wet bricks from wagons and loading them into the kilns, the other pulling the scorching bricks out. They give us gloves once a week, which wear out before a single shift is over. Zeks wind old cloths around their hands but these do not prevent serious burns. Barely a week passes without a zek inflicting an injury on himself to get out of work.

My crippled leg saves me from the kilns. I am sent instead to make fluorescent lamps in a separate workshop. There I make friends with a man who deliberately broke his arm to get away from the kilns. Sanka Mirzaev is a Tatar from Chapaevsk. My wife attended his mother during her numerous pregnancies.

Sanka has had a series of different 'fathers' and eventually ended up in a children's prison where he became very fastidious. He never picks up bread or dog ends from the ground, he will not share a table with a loud or messy eater, and he makes his bed as neatly as a soldier. When his arm starts to heal they threaten to send him back to work in the kilns. Workers who break their arms usually only get a couple of months off. Sanka has plenty of peasant cunning and manages to outwit them by writing a letter to a friend, detailing escape plans. He tries to pass it out via a zek suspected of being a stoolie. The plan works like magic and the letter falls into the Godfather's hands. Sanka is categorised as a potential escapee and banned from the work zone.

Another lad who works with us is so stunted he could pass for a twelve-year-old child. His prison jacket reaches to his toes. "That's our Pakhan,"[26] says Sanka. "Poor little sod. I knew him back in children's camp. His mother was a prostitute. He's never known home-cooking or sweet pies, but he's been sucking on vodka since he was a toddler. His mother used to send him out in the mornings to pick up dog-ends from the streets. Then he had to fend for himself while she entertained her clients. He survived by snatching bread from people's hands, running off and eating it in entranceways. After his mother died of TB, Pakhan took to the streets. He was soon arrested for theft and sent to a children's prison. I got to know him there. I felt sorry for him as he was always being beaten up. Once they stuffed him in a locker and threw him out of a first floor window. Now he's blind in one eye and he can't hear much. One day he stabbed one of his bullies to death. He got six years."

---

26 In criminal jargon a Pakhan is a leader of a gang of thieves. Usually he is a retired thief who sends younger lads out to work for him, a sort of Fagin character.

Instead of becoming feral and cruel as a result of his treatment, Pakhan is withdrawn. He reacts to simple acts of kindness with suspicion. Once I have met my quota I help him finish his and then we get down to the important business of preparing 'Boris Fyodorovich' from industrial 'BF' glue. Pakhan sticks close by my side; unlike the others I don't tease him.

"Pakhan, over here," I call, adding water to the glue and pouring it through a filter. On some days I collect as much as two litres of spirits. It's risky to store the alcohol so we drink it straight away. There are more than enough volunteers. When he has drunk his fill of BF, Pakhan hides under the workbench and goes to sleep wrapped in his jacket.

When Pakhan nears his release date a Toliatti factory sends someone to offer him a job. The emissary is a young Komsomol girl who brings some clothes – several sizes too large for him. He stands sullenly before her looking like a mediaeval courtier in his enormous jacket, the lining bulging through rips. Politely the girl asks: "Are you thinking of taking a correspondence course when you get out of here?"

Too deaf to hear her question, Pakhan cowers in a corner: "It wasn't me! I didn't fucking do it!"

Pakhan is reluctant to leave our company. On the day he is due for release he runs off and hides. We eventually find him huddled under a workshop bench, his thin childish hand gripping a jar of BF. Pakhan looks up at me and smiles his toothless grin: "Ivan, wouldn't it be fucking wonderful if we could feel like this all the time?"

8

On the road

The 1970s

Everyone leaving camp plans to find a good job, marry, get ahead, and of course, never end up inside again. I don't suffer from these illusions, but nevertheless I worry about what I'll do after my release. I have nowhere to live in Chapaevsk and my former plant is refusing to take me back. To apply anywhere else with a passport like mine[27] is not a cheerful prospect. Some of the lads who are up for release ask me to come and live with them, but it's clear how that will end up. I dream of a life as a lighthouse-keeper or a watchman at an observatory. I want to go somewhere far away from so-called civilization, deep in the taiga where there are no Party organizations or vodka shops. Remembering how peaceful I felt in the forest looking after Yura's bees I decide to seek out a similar kind of existence, far away from Chapaevsk.

"I'm never going back to work," I announce to Sanka and VV. "I've inhaled enough chlorine and buried too many workmates. It's a pointless life. Everyone says they'll do their ten years[28] and

---

27 Prison records were written in internal passports which had to be shown when applying for a job or a place to live.

28 After ten years in a hazardous job a worker was entitled to early retirement.

then get out, but by then another kid has arrived or they need money to buy a TV set. I'm not going down that road. I'm sick of being told how to live."

"And how exactly are you going to make your protest? As soon as you open your mouth you'll go straight back inside," VV points out.

"Well, if I don't protest openly at least I won't lift a finger to help the system. Anyway, it'll only be a matter of time before I start to drink again and that'll lead me straight back to the LTP. I'm going south to pick up casual work. In the countryside I'll be free to do more or less as I like. Country people stick more closely to the old ways."

VV turns to Sanka: "So Vanya is going to become a Wanderer.[29] Perhaps you think our beloved Comrade Brezhnev is the Antichrist?"

"The very same."

"And our Founder and Teacher, Comrade Lenin?"

"The Father of Lies,"

"The Communist Party of the USSR?"

"The vessel of Satan."

"And all who submit to its authority?"

"Devil's spawn!"

"But this is not the nineteenth century," VV points out. "Our Russian people don't support vagabonds and holy fools with the generosity of bygone years. How are you going to live?"

"I'll register with a collective farm. No one expects you to work there. The farm will give me a bed and food and my time will be my own. Whenever I get sick of it I can take to the road,

29 A Christian sect that had its roots in Catherine the Great's reign. Followers led a nomadic life in the forests of Russia, refusing to co-operate in any way with the civil and ecclesiastical authorities.

if the police pick me up my papers will say I'm a collective farm worker. Vassya-Honeycake told me there are plenty of farms in the Kuban eager to take people on."

VV bursts out laughing: "All over the USSR peasants are busting a gut trying to leave the farm. You only find old women, drunks and mental defectives there now, and you want to run away *to* a collective farm!"

"There's nothing left for me here. I no longer have a family. These days I'm responsible to no one."

"But you can't run away from yourself," says VV.

"I'm not trying to. All I want to do is get away from everyone who knows me. Especially my mother."

I have sworn never to return home to my parents. While I was inside I learned that my younger brother Sashka died after drinking tainted samogon on New Year's Eve. He came home and fell into a coma in front of my mother and stepfather who were both too drunk to notice their son's condition. By the time they sobered up it was too late to call an ambulance. Perhaps no hospital could have saved him; all the same I blame my parents for Sashka's death.

VV and I are released together. We got on well in jail but on the outside our differences begin to show. No doubt his important mother will find him some easy work – and no doubt he'll soon start taking pills again. Still, he lends me money for a ticket to Sochi.

Before I leave Toliatti I go back to Barkovka to meet Sanka on his release day. I know no one else will come for him so I bring a coat and some clothing to spare him the shame of going home in a prison jacket. Sanka's family live not far from the hostel where I'm staying. He invites me up to meet them.

A heavily pregnant woman opens the door. Fat rolls from her neck to her knees. She squints hard at us for a minute and then throws her arms around Sanka: "Tolik! You're home. Oi! Grish… get a bottle, our lad's back."

Inside the flat youths and girls in various states of drunkenness are draped over chairs and boxes. A few of them turn indifferently to stare at us. Sanka's Heroine Mother waddles up to a comatose man and punches her huge fist into his ear. "Grish, I said wake up you prick-for-legs. Our Misha's back. Give him a drink."

I fear that Sanka will not enjoy the taste of freedom for long.

***

I take a train to Sochi and spend a few weeks wandering along the Black Sea coast, picking up odd jobs. I fall in with other tramps who help me to find places to sleep. We prefer the warmth and companionship of railway stations but the police come round continually waking us up. Sometimes we sleep on stationary trains in sidings but local youths barge through the carriages, taking money off those too drunk to resist.

An older tramp shows me how to make some money by standing in the ticket queue for the Sochi hydrofoil and selling my place to latecomers. This man thinks I'm really wet behind the ears, although I've been a Decembrist and a zek. "How can you reach the age of 35 and not know what a spets[30] is? They have them in all big cities and railway stations. If you get picked up without documents they throw you in for 30 days while they cook up something really incriminating against you. Three times in the spets earns you a year in camp."

I nearly fall victim to this law in the town of Tuapse. A policeman scrutinizes my passport, decides he doesn't like my

---

30 '*Spetsialnii priyomnik*': a lock-up for petty criminals.

face and tears up my document under my nose. Then he arrests me for travelling without a passport. At the police station I try to explain what their colleague has done. They laugh and slap my face a few times. Fortunately they are too lazy to do the necessary paperwork to give me 30 days. Probably they've exceeded their quota of tramps in jail that month.

I have 24 hours to leave town. From Tuapse I board the steamer *Admiral Nakhimov* and sit in the buffet completely indifferent to whether it is taking me north or south. It docks at Novorossisk where I earn a few roubles by carrying boxes of flowers from the pier to taxis. Having money in my pocket at the beginning of the day buys me a breakfast of beer fortified with essence of dandelion. At night I sleep among the feet of giant sailors hurling grenades and charging fascists with bayonets. It might be a Hero City, but its monuments are very draughty.

The town of Novorossisk is the most important oil terminus in the USSR. Vessels from all over the world dock here. I stick to the local port as I know the foreign quays are crawling with plain-clothes police.

A young lad approaches me at a beer-stall, saying he has some business to discuss. Something about him makes me suspicious. Before I have a chance to walk away a police car pulls up and takes me to the spets. My appearance must have given me away.

The spets is a row of cells in the courtyard of the town police station. Eight to ten men are crammed into each stuffy cell. We spend our days playing draughts with bread counters and brewing chefir. A skilled chefirist needs only four sheets of newspaper to kindle a fire that will brew a litre. We have to keep the smoke to a minimum in order not to give ourselves away.

Amongst the guards are a pair of Adyghe twins who are much

more humane than the rest. They give me some cardboard with which I make chess pieces. One of them suggests a game but he plays badly and I win with ease. One of my cell-mates whispers: "Idiot – maybe you should try to lose."

And so I do. It puts the Adyghe in such a good mood he later throws two loaves of bread into the cell. The next day he gives me a mugful of samogon.

That afternoon my chess game is interrupted by shrieks from the courtyard. I stick my head out of the ventilation hole in our cell door and see the police bringing in five girls. One of them, a tall girl with a shaven head, is wriggling between the Adyghe twins and trying to pinch their cheeks. They duck their heads in embarrassment. A camera stands ready in the yard. The bald girl saunters over and stands in front of it, striking exaggeratedly glamorous poses. "Hey, you bastards, get a fucking move on, it's cold out here!"

"Come on, Vera, stop pissing about," says the police photographer.

"And what are you staring at?" she catches sight of me.

I pull my head back into the cell as my mates laugh. It hurts me to hear obscenities fall from the lips of such a young and pretty girl.

The girls have been arrested for picking up foreign sailors. The police threaten to tell their workplaces and schools of their 'crimes.' Those who show fear are blackmailed by the police for sexual favours; those who can't produce documents are put in the women's cell next to ours. It is never empty.

We shout over to each other and pass food and cigarettes across by bribing the guards. Usually the girls have more to give than us poor tramps.

From time to time a fight blows up in the girls' cell. They need to relieve their tension somehow. Vera can't exist for one minute without trying to start a fight. Perhaps having her head shaved has traumatised her. They say it is to get rid of lice, but really it's because it is harder for bald girls to work. Clients are suspicious of their state of health.

I savour my daily exercise in the courtyard, it restores my spirits to look at the sky, hear the noises of the town and feel the rain on my face. One day an elderly man falls into step beside me. He introduces himself as Uncle Misha the Railwayman.

"It's my first time in the spets. It was my own bloody fault for getting drunk and going to the end of the line. In all my 60 years I've never made that mistake. They defrocked me – took away my cap and hammer."

Uncle Misha is a robber who works the railway lines. "I began my career in the 1920s. I was an orphan - my parents died in the civil war. I soon learned that stations are the best places for stealing. People are tightly packed together and they don't know their surroundings. I got caught a few times but no one handed me in. People would rather beat me up themselves and leave the authorities out of it. I guess they had their reasons.

"Then I learned how to rob goods wagons. I climbed onto their roofs and let myself down inside. I'd pick what I wanted, jump off the train and sell my haul to a fence. The only tricky parts were keeping an eye out for the guards and jumping off the moving trains. You have to be fit for that." He glances at my leg.

"When I got older I found a job on the railways. It didn't last long, but I kept my cap and hammer, the tools of my trade. Since then trains have been my home. I know every station in the USSR. Even the smallest country halt. When I get off at a station the first thing I do is study the timetable. I learn them by heart, both summer and winter versions. They're my daily bread."

I laugh. "You remind me of George Peters, a man I read about in a book. He avoided the police thanks to his excellent knowledge of train times."

Uncle Misha opens his toothless mouth in disbelief: "Did you really read that?"

"Yes, it's in a book by an American writer, O. Henry."

Uncle Misha whistles: "Whew! I never thought you could learn a thing from books. Everything in them I already shat out the day before yesterday!"

He takes a surreptitious puff on a roll-up cupped in this hand. "Sometimes I notice a lonely-looking suitcase. Then I wait for everyone to fall asleep. But it drives me mad when some bloody intellectual takes out a book and reads. You can't tear him away. It's like trying to snatch a baby from its bottle. But it also works the other way. A man might bury himself in the book so deep you could stuff him up the arse and he'd never notice. So there's a use for books all the same.

"When everyone's asleep I get down to business. I grab the case, jump off the train, hide alongside it and wait for the next express. Two or three minutes before it leaves I push the suitcase into an axle-box with my long hammer and then climb inside a carriage. I sit in an empty place, wearing my railway cap so the conductor won't ask to see my ticket.

"When he's passed by I start to tell the other passengers stories that I've picked up on my travels. They're always willing to share their food in return for the entertainment. When I've eaten my fill and slept a bit I get out at a suitable stop.

"In any new town the first thing I do is memorise the

timetable. Then I go to the nearest beer shop for a few drinks. After that I collect empty vodka bottles - only the cleanest ones, mind. I take them out somewhere quiet on the edge of town and fill them with water. I use my bootlaces to close the caps. Then I wait till evening and go back to the station. I wander along the platform with a bottle in my hand and almost always get lucky. My bottle reminds passengers they're thirsty so they call out: 'Oi, mate! Where can I get one?'

"'Not far from here, not far at all. About half a kilometre,' I tell them.

"The shop might as well be on the moon. The greedy wretches beg me to sell the bottle. I hum and haw until the train is about to depart and then I give in. They even want to tip me. 'No, no, you're all right,' I say to them. As soon as their train starts I hop on one going in the opposite direction."

I lie awake listening to Uncle Misha snoring beside me. He revolts me. I wonder how he can take advantage of people's trust and their simple desire to drink. I think about it for a long time before concluding that his crimes are nothing new. People deceived others like that even before the revolution.

***

The June dawn breaks at 4am. I awake to find I've run out of matches so I go to get a light from the joggers who are already pounding the sand. To my annoyance everyone turns out to be a non-smoker. Damn sportsmen.

I notice an ugly, squint-eyed fellow studying me.

"Got a light, mate?" I ask, "I've been looking for one for an hour."

"I don't smoke," but he adds, "I drink, though."

He picks his jacket off the ground to reveal a bottle of cognac.

"A man after my own heart!" I cry. "Wait five minutes while I get a light. I want a smoke so badly my arse is dizzy!"

"Go ahead. I'll be here!" he says, pulling his jacket back over the bottle. When I return we silently pass the bottle back and forth between us, each trying to take smaller and smaller mouthfuls. It's early morning and the shops won't open for a long time. We introduce ourselves.

"I'm from Kuibyshev."

"And I'm from Tambov," he says, although his plastic cap proclaims: *I am from Sochi!*

"Could you be the Tambov Wolf?"

"I could be. And what's your name?"

"Hodja Nasreddin."[31]

Tambov Wolf laughs. "Oh, Hodja Nasreddin, why do you wear such a high collar on your jacket?"

"To protect my neck from the sun."

"And if the sun is shining in your face?"

"I turn around and walk in the other direction. Where did you get the cognac?"

"Ask me something easier," replies Tambov Wolf. He pulls a three-kopeck piece out of his pocket and says, as though pronouncing Newton's fourth law of physics: "One coin does not clink."

"And two do not make the right sound." I produce another coin from my pocket.

"Another eight and we'll be OK," he says. I pull all the small change out of my pocket, but he takes only two kopecks from me.

---

31 *Tales of a Sufi* wise man called Hodja Nasreddin, believed to have lived in the thirteenth century, are part of the folk wisdom of Turkic speaking peoples. In this case Ivan and Tambov Wolf are telling each other that they are vagabonds.

"But you said eight," I point out.

"Quite right. Two kopecks and six o'clock in the morning make eight."

The shops open at six. The sun has risen above the horizon so we only have to wait a while longer. However, alcohol is not sold before 11 o'clock. The battle against alcoholism is in full swing and the masses have to be prevented from getting tanked up before work.

At six Tambov Wolf joins the crowd of grandmothers by the shop doors. After a few minutes he emerges and disappears behind the monument to drowned fishermen, signalling for me to follow. We sit down on the nearest bench. From his pocket Tambov Wolf pulls out the sister of the bottle we split earlier and a quarter of a loaf of bread.

"For breakfast," he says. "Don't argue, the bread was come by honestly. The bottle I picked up in passing, to give us something to wash it down with."

"I couldn't do that," I say.

"You don't need to. We have enough."

When I took to the road I made a pledge that I would never steal or get into a fight. That would keep me out of jail, leaving me free to wander until I grew tired of the life. I soon realised that was naive. Christ himself couldn't have wandered the USSR unmolested. His attitude, 'take therefore no thought for the morrow' would have earned him a year at least, so there was not much hope for the rest of us poor sinners. And sinners we certainly are. We all smoke and curse and most of us drink.

Later Tambov Wolf goes off to steal another bottle, this time from a different shop. We drink it, fall asleep on the beach, and the next day he's gone.

***

"Vanya! Got a ciggie, darling?" The prostitute Vera is sitting on a bench sporting a black eye.

As it happens I have. Vera is in an unusually calm mood. As we sit smoking side by side she begins to talk: "I was a trainee draughtsman before the Komsomol got hold of me. Some activists picked me up by the beach, saying that because my dress buttoned down the front I was obviously a prostitute. They hauled me in. Sentenced me as a Decembrist. I had to clean the toilets in the station. When my fifteen days were up I decided I might as well practise what they thought I did anyway. I certainly make a lot more money this way."

She finishes her cigarette. "I'll be off to work now. Thanks for the smoke, love. You tramps are okay."

"Well you won't find any moralists among us."

***

It is time I found a place on a farm. I go down to the town's labour exchange where they direct me to a collective farm about 20 kilometres out of town. I set off in the hot sun and hitch a ride part of the way in a truck. However, it turns out that the farm administration don't want to take anyone on. I am annoyed at the waste of time. I haven't had a hair-of-the-dog and my hands are beginning to shake. Not knowing what to do next, I leave the office and look around. There is a lad standing a little way off. Judging by his appearance he's some sort of tramp like me. He ambles over to where I stand.

"Brother, do you know what time it is?" I ask.

"Five to whatever the fuck you like. You late for work?"

"Work's not a wolf. It won't run off into the forest."

"But I would, given half a chance."

"What're you waiting for? Let's go."

We set off for the distant forest. On the way we swipe salt and paper napkins from the farm's dining room. We pull up some young potatoes and pick a few cucumbers from a field on the outskirts of the farm. I don't regard this as theft. We never take more than what we can eat at one sitting. In private fields we dig into the soil on one side of the potato plants and pull off a few tubers. Then we pack the earth back, knowing that by autumn the plant will yield as many potatoes as its neighbours. Given the tons of fruit and vegetables that rot away in the fields it would be a sin not to take some.

Once we reach the forest we light a fire in a clearing and bake our potatoes. There's no shortage of kindling in the dense and tangled undergrowth. It is good to sit by the fire. I wonder why I've hung around towns for so long. I must have forgotten that you don't need much in this life.

My companion, whose name is Yura, is not talkative. That suits me. I'm happy just to look into the flames. The potatoes bake quickly. We pull them out and toss them from hand to hand until they cool down. They burn in the mouth but the cucumbers soothe our tongues. I decide not to return to the town.

"Yura, where are you headed?"

"Armavir. Let's go together."

"But I can't walk as fast as you."

"I'm in no hurry. Summer's only just begun. Time enough to get there by winter."

"Let's go then."

First we go back to the farm. An old Cossack woman gives us three roubles and a bottle of samogon in return for chopping wood. We ask her for an aluminium mug and a handleless saucepan, and then we take more salt and a glass from the farm's dining room. In the shop we buy tea, tobacco and matches. Beyond the farm we head east, following the sun. All around us are plantations of apricot and cherry trees. When the day draws to a close we lie down by a stream in a grove of willows and black poplars. We fetch some hay from a field and spread it out for a bed.

Yura comes from Dnepropetrovsk and has been on the road for two years. He has already been in the spets twice and wants to avoid a prison sentence. He intends to stay in the Kuban till autumn and then head off into Central Asia. That idea appeals to me and we decide to stick together. We will stay where we are for the summer, keeping our heads down and avoiding any trouble with the law. That means not showing our faces in towns and not stealing.

I am unable to steal in any real sense; I couldn't imagine breaking into someone's house or pickpocketing. As for other sorts of theft – well, everyone in the Soviet Union steals. Our system turns us into thieves. In other countries the most hardened thief knows in his heart of hearts that he's doing wrong. Even as he's hauled off to jail he knows that he deserves his punishment. He may not like it but he knows it is just. You have to answer for your deeds. In the USSR, however, everything is turned on its head. We think someone a fool if he does not steal from the state. The authorities think so too. They pay us so little that we have to steal. That way they encourage us to get our hands as dirty as theirs. Then we're in no position to complain about them, the much greater thieves.

Everyone knows the difference between genuine theft and taking back what has been stolen from us in the first place. We're only expropriating the expropriators.

"Yura," I say aloud, "stealing might be wrong, but when the state steals freedom and takes away human dignity, then people begin to construct their own values."

Yura interrupts me: "Right. And what if everyone invented their own values? What would we have then?"

"Chaos!" I have to admit it.

Yura sleeps. I draw away from the glow of the fire in order to see the stars. I pile up some hay and lie down. I am not drunk. There's even a drop of samogon left for my morning hair-of-the-dog. With everything taken care of, I relax and start to think about how to live my life in a way that will have some sort of meaning. My attitude to the world around me is changing. My youthful dreams of setting the world on fire have died. I know I will never walk to the North Pole or discover a new chemical element. On the other hand I am less disturbed by my crippled leg. I've learned that strength, whether mental or physical, is a cruel and destructive force. Even if you do not intend to use your strength for evil purposes it makes no difference in the end.

After gazing for a long time at the constellations, I come to a decision. I will never again say, 'If only everyone did as I did,' or, 'If only everyone were like that... .' I have to accept that people will never be the way I want them to be.

I am disillusioned with humanity but I cannot not say I hate it. You can hate flies and cockroaches, you can love bees and cabbage pasties, but I don't see how you can love or hate 'people' when they are all so different. The man who says 'I love people' is either a politician or a scoundrel, which are one and the same, or simply an idiot who doesn't know what he's talking about. In the course of my life I've come into contact with tens of thousands of human beings. Some were fine and others I wouldn't have cared to meet in hell. Most were harmless enough. It's unlikely that I myself have caused joy to leap in many hearts.

I decide that from now on I will behave as though other people do not exist. Even when I'm in a crowded bazaar I will act as though I'm on a desert island. To live in and for oneself sounds very simple but in practice it is almost impossible. I am human like anyone else and affected by those around me. Added to which, as a Soviet citizen, I've drunk in the word 'we' with my mother's milk. But whether I succeed or not, the most important thing is that I have made my decision. No one can alter it or prevent me from trying to carry it out.

Perhaps I only want to justify my existence, but I don't think of it like that. Let the clever chaps discover complexes according to Freud or Jung. I feel satisfied and fall sleep at last.

You can only sleep through dawn in the forest if you're really tired. As soon as the sun peeps above the horizon, the birds begin twittering so loudly that it's impossible to sleep. Although I don't drop off until the early hours of the morning I awake in a strangely cheerful and optimistic mood. I've become a slightly different person and I feel something good will happen today.

Yura, on the other hand, is sullen. I wonder if he regrets his decision to take me with him. He pulls off his socks and sniffs them, then he lies down again like a dead man until I have brewed chefir, which revives him somewhat. I ask him not to touch the samogon for a while, explaining that I'm frightened of the dt's.

Coming out onto the main road we start hitching. We decide to go to the bathhouse in Armavir. We stink of bonfires and hay and booze. You can't get yourself clean in a river, even with soap. Besides which, a steam bath is always a treat. If the mediaeval world rested on three whales, the tramp's rests on four: railway station; bazaar; police station; bathhouse.

A truck takes us as far as the town of Kropotkin. "We've got to keep out of the town," Yura says. "The Kropotkin police chief doesn't care for tramps. You've heard about him?"

I shake my head.

"He used to be head of a collective farm. Chased out three tramps one day. They snuck back and stole his geese. Then they wrote a request to Moscow radio 'on behalf of the farm labourers of Armavir' for the well-known and popular song: *Goodbye geese, goodbye!* A couple of weeks later the 500 voices of the Piatnitsky choir reminded the farmer that his geese had been nicked."

"What did he do?"

"Left his farm and joined the Kropotkin police force. Now he takes his revenge on passing tramps." Yura gives a rare smile. "Vagrants all over the country still send their requests to Moscow. Even those in prison."

Yura and I are on the road for more than a month, wandering in a circle around the Kuban. The southern earth nurtures us like a kind mother. You can't take a step without squashing a ripe apricot or a bunch of grapes. All around is a sea of corn and fields overflowing with melons that no one bothers to pick. After they've met government sowing targets farm managers relax and let the harvest take care of itself.

I do not listen to a radio or read a paper. I don't care whether we have cosmonauts in space or receptions for Fidel Castro. My body feels rested and my soul is at peace. No one is nagging at me to work harder or stop drinking.

Then a chill, incessant rain begins to pour down. For three days we barely stick our noses out of a haystack. Once or twice we go up to the nearest farm, where peasants give us as much milk as we want. Yura drinks until his stomach barrels out so tightly you could snap fleas on it with your fingernails.

The rain gets me down. I suggest we take shelter by registering ourselves on a farm. We trudge six muddy kilometres to the nearest farm administration centre and are immediately hired. Yura is sent to tend the cattle while I, as an invalid with no documents except a certificate of graduation from the Novorossisk spets, am hired as a watchman. I patrol at night, shooting in the air to scare off the stray dogs that try to dig up carcasses of diseased cattle from their burial pit. I also have to drive the carthorses out from the stables when the farmers need to take goods to market.

The cattle live in terrible conditions. They don't have enough to eat because feed is expensive. If they get fed at all it's only because the farmers feel pity for the animals. It smites your heart to hear three hundred cows mooing from hunger while the cowhands lie paralytically drunk. In the morning farmers tip sugar beets onto the still-frozen earth of the cattle-pen. The starving cows push and shove to get at the food, trampling their own calves into the filth. When the sun rises and softens the ground the animals wallow up to their bellies in mud and excrement. Still, they're not my responsibility and my job is easy enough.

The local Cossacks treat us cautiously at first. Like all country people they do not broadcast their scandals to strangers. I soon notice they steal everything they can carry. At five in the morning they stumble out of their huts, stuffing empty bags into their pockets. They pile into buses that roar off down the sawdust-strewn road. In the evenings they return with bags full of feed, corncobs, or whatever else they've been able to lay their hands on. They say that a wife won't serve her husband dinner unless he brings at least a couple of planks or a piece of fencing back from work with him.

Looking at me sympathetically, one of the Cossack women sighs: "Oh, you poor man!"

"Why do you say that?"

"How d'you survive with a leg like yours?"

"I get by, always have and always will."

"But you can't ride a bicycle."

"Why the hell would I want to do that?"

"But you can't carry much away on foot!"

"But I don't need anything."

She gapes at me as though I was a simpleton. Later I learn that the first thing any peasant does is buy himself a bicycle. Then he goes to the driver of a combine harvester, slips him three roubles and fills up a bag of cut corn-cobs. Even one sack is hard to carry over the shoulder, but two or three can be hung from a bike. He sells the corn in the market for 15 roubles, making the bicycle a machine for printing money. If he does well he uses his profits to buy a motorbike with a side-car which enables him to steal a lot more.

They say that if you stick a shaft in the Kuban soil in spring you'll have a cart growing by autumn. But this fertile agricultural region is going to waste because of the collective farm system. The more intelligent peasants leave the farm for the towns; the more artful join the Party and sit at conferences where they assure each other that everything is under control. The simpler people stay put and drink everything they can lay their hands on.

It is not true that people only work for money. If someone is paid to dig a hole every day and fill it in again he might work for a while but in the end he'll rebel. That is why all our years of communism have produced only 200 million thieves and drunkards.

I sleep in a five-room hut with four other single down-and-outs, plus three families. One of these consists of a couple of drug addicts that we nicknamed Codeine and Codeina. This pair wander around the farm like somnambulists. They have a baby who sleeps all the time, probably addicted through its mother's milk. The couple are supposed to work in the chicken sheds. At night when the birds are blind Codeina grabs half a dozen, binds their beaks with thread and takes them off to Slavyansk to trade for pills with pharmacists.

Codeine takes alternate shifts with me as a night watchman. He often comes over to play cards with us and drink chefir. He gives out pills to those he trusts. The codeine makes us itch and scratch ourselves compulsively.

Amongst us is a young man who is hiding out on the farm for some reason - you don't ask why. Born a Carpathian peasant, he understands everything that concerns agriculture; as regards anything else, he's as thick as a tree stump. Seeing us scratch ourselves, he goes into the next room and painstakingly examines his clothes for lice.

***

I wake up after a long card session and stumble out of the hut. Bumping into Klava, a neighbour from another hut, I ask her the time.

"Eight," she replies.

"How come?" I'm surprised. The sun is already high in the sky.

"With me it's always eight o'clock," Klava bellows, turning her back to me, bending over and throwing up her skirts. Between her bare buttocks she presents me with two holes, one above the other like the figure eight.

Every day Klava and her husband battle each other with pitchforks and mallets. It's amazing that neither manages to kill the other. When drunk Klava bursts into our rooms, throws off our blankets and tries to climb onto one of us. I keep a hoe by my bed to drive her away. When the lads reject her advances she stands outside cursing and throwing stones at our windows.

As a Heroine Mother of the USSR Klava doesn't have to work. Her husband turns up in the fields now and again, just to see what he can steal. The couple have countless children. The little ones crawl around the farm, putting everything from apricots to dog shit in their mouths.

Still, I'm in no position to judge my neighbours. I drink every day. Samogon is as copious as the waters of the Volga. The local peasants distil it from tobacco. In the morning it makes your head ache unbearably, so you have to take a hair-of-the-dog immediately.

I feel as though I'm being sucked into quicksand. A little while longer and I'll never be able to tear myself away from Red Shaft Collective Farm. My pay is better than it was in any chemical factory and there's not much work to do. I enjoy plentiful food, lots to drink and girls as sweet and strong as apples.

The girls came to us from the Cossack village of Petrovka that lies twelve kilometres to the south. They have their fun with us away from the eyes of their fathers and brothers. In their community they count for damn all. Since early childhood they've had to work like donkeys. The breadth and strength of their arms deceives anyone who wants to be deceived. Sometimes in the morning I discover that the girl I've spent the night with is not even 16 years old.

I get caught in a storm while bringing in the horses. In a few seconds I'm soaked to the skin. I develop pneumonia. The farm's doctor wants to take me to hospital, but I refuse.

"You'll be dead by tonight."

"All to the good."

"Do you know what you are saying?"

"Yes. I have to shit, and you're preventing me."

She withdraws. Somehow I make it to the bucket my friends have supplied and then I sleep. In the morning I awaken feeling weak but well and flooded with happiness. I have a strong urge to visit my daughter in Estonia.

A week later I leave the collective farm, taking only the watch they award me for my labour. I don't even collect my wages. Money frightens me.

9

Georgia

I want to see Natasha before she forgets who I am, so I set off for Estonia. A tractor drives me into Slavyansk and I walk to the station. The conductor of a westbound express is happy to give me a berth in exchange for my Red Shaft watch. I travel as far as Rostov; after that I make my way northwards on local trains, keeping an eye on schoolboys who always know when the conductor is on his way. When the train halts and they jump off I limp along after them, climbing into carriages that have already been checked. All the same I'm caught a few times and put off the train. From Rostov I go to Taganrog, and then across Ukraine through the Donbass and back into Russia, through Belgorod, Kursk, Oryol and Tula.

The whole way I keep as sober as glass and on constant lookout for the police. My jacket is only distinguishable from a convict's by its collar, my shoes are falling apart and I sprout a beard. I have only to step into a waiting room for the attention of all uniforms to fasten upon me like a magnet. In Tula I am accosted by a guardian of law and order: "Where are you going?".

"Home."

"And where's 'home'?"

"The collective farm."

"Which collective farm would that be?"

"What d'you mean 'which'?" I look at him with the eyes of Saint Francis. "Ours!"

I tell myself not to overdo it, for the policeman probably left the collective farm himself not so long ago.

"And where is *your* farm?" he spits out the words like pieces of shit from his mouth.

"It's in the Kuban," I put on a southern accent.

"Do you have your documents?"

"Well of course!" I reach into my jacket and pull out a package wrapped in old newspaper. The policeman looks on with distaste as I peel off the paper. My new passport is already stained and the residence permit almost illegible.

"Sorry… I didn't know that it was leaking."

"What was?"

"The lamp!"

"What lamp?"

"The kerosene one. The electrician was drunk and burnt the transformer."

"Get the hell out of here! If I see your stupid face again you'll go straight into the spets."

So I continue northwards, trying to ride by night when ticket controllers are sleepy. By day I wander around towns, collecting empty bottles for a couple of roubles to buy bread. I bum cigarettes, or pick up dog ends and roll them in newspaper. Sometimes I share a cigarette with another vagrant, sitting by his side smoking in silence, feeling as close as brothers.

I reach Moscow, cross the city, and head northwards. As I near my destination I feel my courage fail. I long to see Natasha, but will she be pleased to see her father, especially in his beard and filthy clothes? At Bologoye I wait a whole day for an Estonia-bound train, sitting on a cold platform lost in thought.

As night falls I rise, cross the footbridge and take the next train south. I return to Moscow and then jump trains to Tambov, Rostov and finally to Sochi. I am relieved that I made my decision in time. If I'd seen Natasha I might have done irreparable harm.

***

"Kind people! Answer me anyone who hears!"

"What d'you want?" I call out.

A blind man taps his way towards my voice. His face is exactly as I imagine Blind Pew's in *Treasure Island*. He doesn't wear dark glasses, perhaps because he wants people to see the cruel livid scars around his eyes.

"Brother!" he cries, "Help me get a bottle. I can hear a whole crowd of people around me. I'll be trampled."

Not waiting for my reply, he pours some small coins from his pocket into his cap. "Get us a couple of bottles."

"But I haven't enough for one myself."

"What the hell are you talking about? Take as much as you need! And a bit extra for yourself. My trousers are sagging with the weight. Perhaps you need it all?"

I come out of the shop with three bottles and catch up with Blind Pew on the corner. With his cap held out to passers-by he whines: "Help me good people. I was burned in a tank at the battle of Kursk."

"I see you waste no time," I say.

"Ah, you're back. Well, what are you dithering for? Slurping up the snot dripping from your nose? Where shall we drink?"

"It's all the same to me."

Taking my arm, Pew directs me to left and right, until we

reach an obscure beer stall tucked away under a railway bridge. They instantly lay out glasses for us. Placing a finger across the rim of each glass in turn, Pew carefully pours the wine.

"I grew up in Sochi. I was blinded a few years ago when I fell into a pit of quicklime. Usually I take someone along with me to keep an eye out for the police and to buy bottles. I used to have a girlfriend but the police picked her up in Sukhumi.

"The cops can't do much except give me a kicking, but I'm scared of being sent to the invalid home. It's worse than strict-regime prison. They take your pension and the staff steal all the food. Anyone who still has legs runs away.

"Of course if you live rough you're caught between two flames. In railway stations there's plenty of folk around, but you have to look out for the police. In quiet places you get beaten up and robbed by thugs. They know we won't run screaming to the law. Anyway, where are you headed?"

"Central Asia."

"Why not stick around with me? You'll see how much we can make in a day."

"Sorry, I've made up my mind. The police here are getting on my nerves.'

"Well I want to get to Sukhumi to find my girlfriend. Let's go together."

I agree out of curiosity. Sukhumi is in the right direction.

After we've finished the wine we go to work. Blind Pew directs me to the centre of town and tells me to stop outside the department store. Taking off his cap and putting a sombre expression on what is left of his face, he begins to sing:

The bright moon shone

Over the old graveyard
And the judge wept
by a grey tombstone.

A crowd gathers to hear the sad song of the boy sentenced to death by his own father. I walk from one street corner to the other keeping a lookout for the cops. From time to time Blind Pew tips his takings into his pocket so that people do not think he is making too much. When he points his index finger downwards it means it is time for a smoke-break. Finally Pew says: "Greed killed the friar, let's stop now."

We fortify ourselves with wine and count our takings. A Moscow diva would envy us. In two hours we have made thirty roubles.

"But you only sing one song," I complain.

"It's the only one I can remember."

We buy some bottles for the night. I take Pew home to the basement where I've been dossing but this turns out to be a mistake. His snores not only keep me awake but they must have awoken everyone on the floor above. In the early hours of the morning the police arrive and haul us off. Luckily they give us nothing worse than a beating. We have 24 hours to leave Sochi.

Reaching the station, we walk along a platform and force open the pneumatic doors of a local train. We lie down in an empty carriage and Pew is soon snoring again. A couple of hours later the train jerks and begins to move, taking us towards Sukhumi. I check the adjoining carriage before returning to give Pew the all-clear. He stumbles down the carriage, singing a song I taught him the night before, one I remember from childhood.

Allow me to introduce myself:
my name is Nikolai Bottle
Everyone points their fingers
and calls me 'drunk' and 'wastrel.'

At work they laugh:
"Bottle's drunk all day!"
The boss picks on me
but I'll make him pay!

Again the dt's torture me,
my family's gone; the street's my life.
Vodka is my only friend,
Who introduced us? My wife!

I do not stand with hand held out,
No – I walk through the bazaar
Crying: Good people – buy my soul!
But who wants the soul of a drinker?

My song is a success: people laugh and give Pew money and a glass of chacha.[32] I make no sign that I know him.

By the time we reach Sukhumi, Pew is rejoicing over the money he's made. He asks me to accompany him further, explaining he'll forget the song by tomorrow morning and will need me to teach it to him again.

I decline. To me, begging is degrading, and besides, I don't want to be supported by Pew. When we alight at Sukhumi he directs me to the bazaar. A group of alkashi has gathered by the

---

32 A Georgian spirit.

entrance. One of them, a bloated, ragged woman, gives a screech. Detaching herself from her comrades she runs up and flings her arms around Pew. Together they stagger off to the station to work the train again.

I wander off to try my luck in town. I've never been to Georgia before and I feel out of place. People are better-dressed than in Russia and I sense they're looking down their noses at me. I spend the day wandering through the town drinking nothing but Turkish coffee. The streets are full of men kissing each other and talking across every doorway.[33] Many people have photos of their dead pinned on their lapels and most women wear mourning. Two men begin talking behind me and I step to one side, thinking a fight is about to break out. Cars career like rabid dogs, paying little attention to lights. Drivers stop to chat to friends, ignoring the angry queues behind them

I spend the money Blind Pew left me and then wander back to the bazaar. A market woman beckons me over and asks me to help carry her baskets of peppers. Happy to earn a bit of cash, I begin hauling baskets over to her stall.

"If we see your ugly face again you'll spend the rest of your life working to buy medicine," a voice growls in my ear.

I turn round. A group of Kurds are glaring at me. There is nothing left to do but get the hell out of here.

I haven't gone far before a pot-bellied policemen hisses through gold teeth: "You, Vassya! Come here!"

This is the end of my wandering, I think.

The police station is piled to the ceiling with confiscated mandarins. Three other vagrants are loading them into cars. The police order me to help them. When we're done the cops give us

---

33 Talking across a threshold is considered bad luck in Russia.

each five roubles and a bottle of chacha. I walk out of the station shaking my head in bewilderment. "I won't be able to tell anyone about this," I say to one of the other tramps. "They'll think I'm a compulsive liar. Russian police would sooner hang themselves with their own belts than behave like that."

A dark man approaches me. "Want a job Vassya?"[34]

"What sort of job?"

"Building a fence – three or four days."

"How much?"

"Ten roubles a day and drink."

"Where d'you want me to go?"

"To the village. I'll drive you there and back." The man points to a car.

I haven't much choice so I go along. It's dark when we arrive at the man's village. He takes me to his farm and directs me to a barn where bunches of bay leaves and eucalyptus are drying. He warns me not to smoke: a spark could send the whole place up in flames. I lie down and sleep in the sweet-scented air.

For three days I dig holes, set posts into them and string up barbed wire. The wire scratches and tears my hands even through gloves. An old man lives in the house with three huge dogs. In the evening he puts out flagons of wine and chacha for me. I don't touch the chacha for I know that once I start on it I'll never finish the work.

While I am stretching out the wire I see a Russian working in a neighbouring field. He comes over.

"I've been here two months," he says. They give me all the chacha I want but they never seem to have any money to pay me.

---

34 Vassya is a generic name other nationalities give to Russians. It has the slightly derogatory connotation of 'simple village lad.

Each morning I have to work for my hair-of-the-dog. Then I finish the bottle in the evening. I can't seem to find a way out."

The old man sees us talking and calls me over: "Police coming," he says, making signs that I'll be arrested.

"Okay, give me my money and I'll leave."

"No monny, my son bring monny tomorrow."

I almost cry with rage. I've ripped up my hands for nothing. I know that if I leave without my pay I'll resent it for the rest of my life. The old man stands watching me, surrounded by his dogs. His eyes laugh at me. There is nothing I can say. Unexpectedly even to myself I go into the barn, grab my things and cry out: "If I don't see my money in five minutes I'll burn the place down !"

I show him the box of matches in my fist.

The old man immediately finds the money. Fearing his dogs, I grab a pitchfork, only throwing it away after I have left the farm far behind me.

At Sukhumi railway station I join up with another 'Vassya,' a tubercular lad named Artur. We discuss the difficulties of working in the Caucasus.

"It's worse in the mountain villages," says Artur. "The Svan people lock you up at night. If you try to escape they'll cut off one of your fingers. Even if you make them pay up the villagers take the money back off you as you leave. What can you do when you're alone? They all know each other and the police are their cousins. Yes brother, it's real slavery up there.

"It's true no one forces us to work in the mountains, but we can't earn anything in town. When someone wants to hire me I say to them: 'I'll work for you, only no skullduggery! I have no house or car to lose; you won't have either if I don't get my pay!'

"But I must say there are some really stupid tramps. Some of them only take jobs so they can nose around for something to steal. They grab whatever they can find, run off, sell it, and get picked up right away at the nearest beer-stall."

I don't linger in Sukhumi as I fear the old man's son might find me. I go back to Sochi and my old haunts.

***

My legs are tired after drinking for the whole morning. The woman who sells pies on the sea front has shut her stall and gone off to lunch. I park myself on her stool. Holiday-makers stroll past on their way to the beach. A lad detaches himself from his group: "What you sellin' here, uncle?"

"Jokes!"

"How much you charge?" he asks in an exaggerated peasant accent.

"Roub' each," I answer in the same tone.

"So much!"

"Why, I'm almost giving them away. Roub' if you don't know the joke and I'll give you a roub' if it's already grown a beard."

"Go on then!" The group gather around my stall. I am heavily under the influence of Bacchus and quickly earn 15 roubles, not because my jokes are so good but because the youths are in high spirits and pleased to be entertained.

The next day, after drinking my hair-of-the-dog, I go to collect the baggage I left behind in spring. Much to my surprise, the man who was looking after it has not sold all my things, although he hasn't left much. He gives me a small rucksack in exchange for my suitcase. Into this I put underwear, photographs, two novels and a cloth-bound exercise book in which I write the crosswords that I like to devise during my sober periods.

I set off for Central Asia, where work is easier to find. Luckily most trains run at night so I'm able to sleep on them and spend the days wandering around Sukhumi, Samtredia, Tblisi and Kirovbad. I travel without tickets. Although I have money I think it's as crazy to pay for a ticket as it would be to drive my own Mercedes.

Baku reminds me of Central Asian cities, with its cafes serving black tea in tiny narrow-waisted glasses. But I'm not interested in tea. From first thing in the morning I'm drinking beer and the local Agdam fortified wine.

After quenching my thirst I lean against a wall to watch the local people. A passer-by stops to pick up a crumb of bread from the ground. The man presses the crumb to his lips and places it on top of the wall. "So the birds can reach it more easily," he says, seeing my astonishment, "in Azerbaijan we respect bread, my friend."

In the bazaar I make the acquaintance of some local tramps and together we earn 15 roubles loading a trailer with oranges. Learning that I have nowhere to spend the night they invite me to come with them. "We have a splendid place. Safe as a tank and warm as a bathhouse. The police don't check – it's in the basement of the officers' flats."

We buy several bottles and take the tram across town to our lodging place. Going down to the basement, we open a thick steel door and scramble over the central heating pipes, so hot they turn spit into steam. The shelter is as dark as the Pharaoh's tomb. My new friends light candles and drink themselves to sleep.

I spend the whole night awake, sitting in total darkness after the candles gutter out. I haven't had enough to drink; it takes a lot to give me a couple of hours' oblivion. In this state I daren't even close my eyes or the nightmares will begin. The air around me is heavy with foreboding. I feel like an animal who senses an earthquake approaching. My new acquaintances snore happily while I goggle into the darkness. Rats scurry past. They are not part of my nightmare, for one of my sleeping friends wakes with a yelp: "Bastards! We'll have to bring some sausage tomorrow or they'll grow too bold altogether!" He drops off again.

It seems as though the night will never end. When a radio in the flat above us begins to broadcast morning exercises I feel as joyful as if I'd seen the second coming of Christ. We crawl out of the basement and I part company from my acquaintances forever. "Lads, if that basement were stacked with vodka and it was thirty degrees below outside you'd only get me back in there under armed escort."

"What did you expect? The Astoria?"

"But it's full of rats!"

"So what? Did they eat you alive?"

"Who knows what was on their minds. I'm not hanging around to find out."

I wander off to the port. Sailors stand by the gangplanks of Caspian ferries scrutinising tickets. They turn me back a couple of times as I try to sneak aboard. An Azerbaijani notices my unsuccessful attempts: "Do you want to earn the price of a bottle?"

"What must I do for it?"

"Carry these two suitcases on board this ferry. Your hands will be full so you can tell the controller that someone behind you has your ticket."

But the two suitcases seem too large for me to carry.

"Pick them up, give them a try," urges the Azerbaijani, seeing me hesitate.

The cases are extraordinarily light. "What's in them, cotton wool?"

"Walnuts."

The Azerbaijani has been kicked out of Baku by the local police after they stung him for 50 roubles for illegal trading. I pick up the cases and board the ship without any trouble.

When we dock at Krasnovodsk in Turkmenistan I help the man unload his cases. As we step ashore cops surround us. The Baku police must have radioed ahead to their Turkmen colleagues who have now come to collect their bribe. Ignoring me, they take the Azerbaijani to the station, leaving me with the cases. After waiting several hours for him I go to the market and sell the walnuts for 80 roubles. My lucky day.

In the evening I catch a train to Tashkent, slipping the carriage conductor some money. Like all conductors in Asia he regards the railway as his personal fiefdom, except when it comes to cleaning; then it belongs to the state.

Beyond the windows there is nothing but desolation. The desert may be lovely in spring, but this is winter and there is nothing but an expanse of grey dunes stretching between horizons, unrelieved by grass or bushes. Occasionally the train halts by a few wretched clay hovels with mangy camels tethered behind them.

Ashkhabad may mean beloved city, but it doesn't deserve the name. In the autumn of 1948 it was destroyed by an earthquake so severe that only one building remained undamaged. The town was built afresh, with buildings no higher than three stories. They look as though they were hatched from the same incubator. The streets are only slightly less depressing than those of Krasnovodsk; some are lined with trees but, this being December, it makes little difference.

At the station buffet I fall in with a local alkie called Kerya. Together we banish our hangovers with a bottle of wine then go down to the Tekinskii bazaar. The stock exchange, as the bazaar is called, is a lively place where local alkies congregate. It is easy enough to earn a couple of roubles hauling baskets of apples. As soon as we have a few coins in our hands we take care of our drinking requirements. Only after that do we think of food. We help ourselves to apples, capsicums, Chardzhou melons, and dip our dirty paws into great barrels of marinated garlic.

Kerya shows me a bunch of keys in his possession. "These open all 64 flats in a new apartment block," he says with pride. "It was built by Bulgarians in an international friendship project. I stole the keys from a drunken builder. It's still empty. I've already slept a few nights there. Come home with me. You'll sleep like a lord."

The 'Bulgarian' building protects us from the 20-degree frost outside, but I grow sick of Kerya's company. Drink is his only topic of conversation.

"Where do the other tramps sleep?" I ask. "Do the cops make up feather beds for them in the railway station?"

"Not likely. If they catch you sleeping there they give you a good going over, and if the same cop catches you twice you get a month for sure." Kerya narrows his eyes like a contented cat. "I had to sleep in a basement for nearly three months before I got hold of these keys!"

He reminds me of the legendary Volga tramp who found himself a place under an upturned boat on the beach. Graciously inviting another tramp to come in and doss down beside him,

he placed a pile of dog ends before the man: "Have a smoke, brother, don't be shy. I was in your position myself not so long ago."

"Where did you sleep before you got the keys?" I ask, wanting to prolong this rare conversation.

"Like me to show you?"

"Why not? There's nothing else to do."

Off we go, picking up a few bottles on the way with the remains of my walnut money. Kerya takes me to a shabby block of flats and leads me down to the basement. Although it is night, the scene below is as bright as day, lit by a bonfire of burning tyres. A group of people are sitting around the fire, women as well as men. Their faces are covered in hideous weeping sores produced by a tropical disease that is rife in Turkmenia. The filth in which the tramps live spreads the infection. When the sores heal they leave a deep scar. It is hard enough to behold children suffering from the disease but the tramps look truly repulsive.

Nevertheless, I am pleased at the thought of company so I sit down and produce my bottles. The basement dwellers welcome me as though I was Santa Claus. I'm already three sheets to the wind and after a top-up I feel such a sense of brotherhood that I invite all the tramps over to our Bulgarian house. Kerya drops into a few more basements on the way back. Soon we are about fifty people. We stock up as we go, from every street-corner, bottle-peddling pensioner.

Our Bulgarian house is soon blazing with light and rocking with noise like a Caribbean cruiser gone off course in the night. Some of our guests sing; others recall old offences. Glass windows shatter and curses echo through the rooms. The police arrive before anyone is killed. They drive us out of the building, whacking us enthusiastically with their truncheons as we go. However, they seem reluctant to arrest us, probably through fear of contagion. In the confusion I manage to slip off and make my way back to the station. I've had enough of Ashkhabad.

***

As the train slows to a halt between Artik and Dushak I ask a soldier on the platform: "Can I get off for a smoke?"

With a bored gesture, he points the barrel of his Kalashnikov towards the door. However, as soon as my feet touch the ground he shouts: "Stop! I'm arresting you for breaching frontier regulations." He points a revolver at my head.

A sergeant comes running up and helps escort me to a separate carriage. There is another man already inside it. The soldiers lock us in and leave. I pull two bottles of wine from my rucksack and give one to my companion. We drink quickly before the soldiers return.

Border guards are recruited from the keenest Komsomol activists, the type of person who will happily inform on his colleagues. Someone must have told an officer that we got drunk after our arrest. At Dushak the interrogating officer is very persistent about this. The soldier who arrested me stands by his side looking so miserable that I take pity on him and say that I was already drunk when I stepped off the train.

Then the officer points to my notebook of crosswords. "What are these?"

"Crosswords, I make them up."

"Why?"

"It passes the time. I sent one to *Smena* once," I babble, "but they rejected it with apologies. They said one of my words was derived from Church Slavonic."

"Hmm… Why were you trying to cross the Soviet border?"

"Who me? Do I look like a madman? I don't know a word of Farsi and I can't run."

The officer glances at my leg. I sense that he does not believe I'm guilty. But once the wheels of justice are in motion there is no going back.

'Let's hope no one trod on the judge's foot in the bus,' I think to myself on the morning of my trial. The length of my sentence will depend on the judge's mood. It's obvious I'm not an Iranian spy, but I am a vagrant and idleness is a crime against the very foundation of the Soviet state.

My trial lasts a few minutes. I refuse my right to a final word and this probably pleases the judge, allowing him to get away to his lunch. He gives me a year of strict-regime prison with compulsory treatment for alcoholism. There is no hope of remission. I am not overjoyed with this sentence but neither am I tearing my hair out. By this time I know I can survive camp. I only have to remember not to think myself smarter than the others or get mixed up in other people's business. If I share my tobacco down to the last roll-up and refuse to give way to self-pity then prison life will be tolerable. Still, I feel apprehensive as I await my transfer, wondering what my fellow inmates will be like.

10

Turkmenistan

The prisoner we call Death Number Two glares at me: "Hey, slurper! Are you from Kolyma or what?"

I shake my head. The way you drink your chefir reveals your camp history. 'Kolyma' drinkers swallow their chefir in three gulps; 'Norilsk' drinkers in two.

"Never mind, let's have another brew," Death Number Two picks up his teapot and runs over to the Titan boiler in the corner of our workshop. He rinses the pot, pours in some hot water, sprinkles in a large heap of green tea and runs back to his bench to put the lid on before the tea cools. We huddle together in a circle, smoking rough tobacco rolled in newspaper while we wait for the chefir to brew. The anticipation is even better than the chefir itself. When it is ready Death carefully fills a bowl and pours it back into the teapot, so that the leaves settle and do not get into our mouths.

"Have a punch in the liver, Vanya," Death hands me a cup.

I have to dope myself with chefir or I won't be able to do a day's work. I feel like death myself when I awake in the morning. My head and muscles ache, my guts churn and my skin crawls. After a few mouthfuls of chefir I return to life. I team up with a group of fellow chefirists, for only the very strong or the completely despised can survive on their own.

The huge workshop buzzes like a million beehives. Dust and tobacco smoke hang so thick you can see no further than ten metres. The midday heat rises to 45 degrees so everyone strips to the waist. Bodies gleam with sweat as they bend over their sewing machines.

I work on my own machine, making gloves. This is almost freedom as it saves me from the production line. I can work at my own pace and it is not hard to meet the quota of 72 pairs a day. My pay goes straight to the camp for my keep. The few roubles I earn for exceeding the quota pay for tobacco and tea. Prisoners with wealth and influence buy their quota from other zeks. Freed from the obligation to work, they lounge about smoking opium and hashish.

Most of Ashkhabad's 1,500 inmates take opium. It is brought in by visitors, delivery-men or sometimes thrown over the fence at a pre-arranged spot. Even the guards will bring in drugs for a large enough bribe. Indian hemp grows in the camp yard. As soon as the buds appear they are picked, dried and smoked in joints.

You can buy drugs in the camp bazaar along with anything else you need. Zek traders set up stalls outside the barracks and sell envelopes, stamps, tobacco, tea, socks and even tomatoes, potatoes and rice. Some of the Turkmen zeks never use the canteen, preferring to cook their own pilaus on bonfires outside the barracks. You can always supplement your diet with cans of condensed milk, traded for opium by tubercular addicts who have climbed over the fence from the hospital zone.

The Turkmen and Uzbeks swallow their opium with green tea. Sometimes they spear a ball on some wire and heat it over a flame. Then they put their heads under a newspaper funnel to inhale the smoke. When a powerful Turkmen is due for release he cooks up a big pilau and stirs in opium and hashish. Friends take their turns with the spoon in strict pecking order.

An old Turkmen is brought into our cell. As soon as the guards have left he shuffles into a corner, squats down and begins to sing endless plaintive dirges. As he sings he rocks back and forth on his heels, sometimes so violently that he keels over onto the floor. He seems to be a lunatic, but we begin to suspect that the old Turkmen *babai* is in fact as high as a kite. Everyone racks their brains trying to work out how he got hold of his drugs. He would have been carefully searched so he couldn't have brought them in from the outside. We keep a close watch on the old man and notice that every so often he breaks off his lament, chews on the sleeves of his caftan, then rolls his eyes heavenwards and resumes his keening. After hours of questioning he confides in another Turkmen zek that he was forewarned of his arrest and so he prepared himself by boiling up opium and soaking his clothes in the solution.

When the rest of the cell discovers the secret of the *babai* they tear off his caftan, rip it to shreds and eat it. Everyone is off their heads for the next two days. I try a bit but it has little effect on me; I have not acquired a taste for opium.

"Death," I remark, "it seems the Turkmen can sing for 24 hours a day and about anything at all. If he sees a camel train passing, he'll sing,

The first camel goes by,
The second goes by,
The third goes by…

"When the whole train has passed he sings,

> *And at the back a little camel goes by,*
> *And blood drips from his hooves.*
> *Oh! If only someone could see him!*
> *They would weep tears of pity!*

"I have never heard one cheerful song. They're all mournful."

"Ah," replies Death, "people say the Italians are the songbirds of the world, but they're nothing compared to the Turkmen. They don't speak much; their philosophy is all in their songs."

***

Most of Ashkhabad's inmates have been sentenced for drug-related crime. Almost every Central Asian adult smokes hashish but there are far fewer addicts among them than amongst the Russians and other Europeans. For centuries the locals used hashish and raw opium but widespread addiction only appeared with the Russians.

As most of Turkmenistan is desert, drugs are brought in from Kyrgyzia, which has a more favourable climate for hemp and poppies. Whole villages are devoted to their cultivation. Smugglers also bring in drugs from Iran and Afghanistan. The mafia who control the narcotics trade don't usually take drugs themselves and mostly employ outsiders as couriers. Although the police are astonishingly inefficient, they have to catch a few smugglers, which makes it a dangerous business. You get five years for a small quantity and 15 for larger amounts. You might even be shot.

A man called Lazarev works on a machine near me. Although

he comes from a family of Old Believers[35] he's been a tramp and an alcoholic for much of his life. Lazarev tells me how he ended up in camp. "One day a guy came up to me at a beer stall and bought me some drinks. We got talking and he asked if I wanted to make some money.

"'Sure,' I said, 'how?'

"'Take a suitcase to Frunze. We'll give you your ticket and the key to a locker in the station. There'll be 1,000 roubles inside.'

"Of course I had a pretty good idea what was in the case but I asked no questions. I hoped that the money would help me clean up and go back home to my wife. The man bought me a new suit of clothes and took me to the barbers. I reached Frunze without being stopped by the police. When I opened the locker I found only 200 roubles and a kilo of opium. I thought I could at least try to sell the opium, so I left the suitcase in the locker and walked out of the station. The police were waiting for me around the corner and I got eight years. The mafia have to throw them a fish now and again.

"It would've been worse for me if I'd held on to the suitcase. I didn't know then that the courier is always tailed, like in a spy story. There's a lot of money at stake. If a courier runs off he's followed onto a train and when he goes out to the open platform for a smoke he's pushed off. The blind Chechen in hut number four had his eyes gouged out. He tried to double-cross the mafia. After they'd finished with him they handed him over to the police."

Listening to Lazarev I realise I could easily have been tricked in the same way. In Baku I agreed to carry walnuts onto the ship

---

35 The Old Believers were a sect that broke away from the Russian Orthodox Church in the seventeenth century. Members were supposed to renounce alcohol and tobacco.

without looking inside the cases. I took tomatoes from Margilan to Tashkent for the price of a ticket. I'll be less naive in future.

Inside the camp the unfortunate Lazarev became addicted to opium. He needs two balls each day, but he can never earn enough on the sewing-machines to buy them. In his spare time he makes syringes from small glass tubes taken from light-bulbs. The plunger is a wooden stick and the stopper made of rubber cut from the soles of his boots. He buys needles from craftsmen who make them from tin cans in the metal workshop. Syringes are scarce in the camp and Lazarev is in demand. Several times a day an addict comes up to him to prepare a fix. First they put a ball of opium in an empty penicillin container, fill it with water and boil the mixture over a burning wick. When the opium dissolves the needle is inserted and the solution sucked up into the syringe. As the drug is mixed with coffee, clay and all sorts of impurities it is filtered through a piece of cotton wool. Lazarev collects the cotton-wool filters, boils them up and injects himself, weeping in frustration as he stabs the needle into his ruined veins.

Conditions in the camp are so filthy that drug users drop like flies. Addicts share needles with syphilitics and TB sufferers. A night never passes without some deaths. In one night eighteen prisoners die from injecting adulterated drugs. The supplier is never discovered but we all know that the tragedy occurred because the dealer was in debt. Addicts know the risks they run but almost no one comes off the needle.

The most powerful zeks always find out in advance when the son of a Party family is coming in. They wait eagerly for the young innocent, ready to envelop him with care and attention. When he arrives they ply him with tobacco and tea and allow him to win at cards. They stage situations where he is threatened by thugs so that they can step in and save him. They fill him with drugs until he's convinced of his invulnerability. Then everything comes crashing down around his ears. He loses heavily at cards and his comrades insist he pays up. He writes home pleading for money to be sent in. As long as he can pay he survives. When they have wrung all they can from their victim the criminals leave him without drugs or protection, and he's lucky if they don't rape him into the bargain.

The Ashkhabad Godfather needs neither the SVP nor stool-pigeons. When he wants information he puts two or three of the more powerful addicts in the isolator and keeps strict watch to make sure no drugs get in. In two days he knows everything. As long as the Godfather knows who's dealing no one is touched. The authorities get their bribes and everything is under control. As soon as anyone steps out of line they are punished. This happens, for example, when someone tries to do a bit of dealing on the quiet and doesn't give a percentage to the guards.

***

"I want nothing more to do with drug addicts," I tell Death Number Two. "I've seen enough of them in here."

The addicts act as though they've discovered some divine secret beyond the reach of ordinary mortals, as though drugs have opened their eyes and shown everything in its true light. Yet in fact they are even more degraded than us alcoholics. They are capable of any treachery to get hold of their ball of opium.

I am not trying to justify alcoholism. I know men who have drunk away their families, their homes and their jobs. I see one of them in the mirror every time I shave. But a drug addict would sell his mother and introduce his sister to the needle so that she has to prostitute herself to buy drugs. The difference between us is that an alkie who sells his last shirt for a bottle wouldn't hesitate to give a glass to a friend; a drug addict would never do the same. Alkies can leave a bottle in someone's care for a while, knowing it won't be touched. No addict would let even his best friend look after his drugs. They hide their stuff away and begrudge their friends even a tiny piece. In the camp they grow their nails long, hoping to get an extra scraping themselves, all the while eyeing their friends' nails with suspicion. No, there can be no comradeship among addicts, whereas an alcoholic will always find someone at the beer-stall to tie his belt to his glass for him, to steady his hand, or tip the glass to his trembling lips.

If I'm honest I have to admit my first prison sentence was due to my pill habit, but I don't consider myself a drug addict. My passion for alcohol is enough. I would have to take up crime to be able to afford drugs and I'm not capable of that. Vodka, on the other hand, is always around, it's cheap, and if the worst comes to the worst I can go without it.

Many alcoholic zeks drink 'chimirgess' which is distilled in the joinery shop from enamel paint. They mix it with water and then strain it to obtain a clear liquid. Anyone who drinks it goes completely off his head but if he's taken to hospital and breathalysed there'll be no reaction at all. In fact there's not a drop of alcohol in chimirgess, and so I'm not attracted to it.

There's a Gypsy in our work brigade called Pashka Ogli. He's so skinny we call him 'Death Number One.' Pashka is not like the other Gypsies who are proud and keep to themselves. Everyone laughs at Pashka for his strange ways. Hearing that once upon a time aristocrats used to drink champagne from ladies' slippers, he fills one of his stinking boots with chimirgess and drinks it down. "As pure as tears," he sighs and collapses in a corner.

Pashka stands by my machine, turning gloves inside out so I can sew them more quickly. He never meets his own quota but I pay him for helping me.

"Vanya," he remarks one day. "You know they watch us all the time in here. They even check the books we borrow from the library."

"Don't be stupid. Maybe in some political prisons but not in ours. They're not interested."

"You don't know what you're talking about."

He shows me volume 18 of Lenin's *Collected Works*, which he has tucked into his waistband. When an officer comes into view Pashka opens his Lenin. Taking a pencil from behind his ear he starts to underline and make exclamation marks in the margins. He buttonholes the officer and plies him with idiotic questions on Marxist-Leninism. Soon even the camp's political instructor is giving Death Number One a wide berth. Everyone thinks Pashka an idiot, but I am not so sure.

***

"See him over there?" Death Number One points to a bull-necked man working in the next row from ours, muscles bulging as he pushes gloves through his machine. "He's known as 'Cannibal.' He escaped from a Kolyma camp in the 1950s. He and his mate took a fatted calf with them. They fed up the young lad before their escape and then killed him when their supplies ran out. Can you imagine them, patting him on the shoulder in encouragement in order to feel the extra flesh on him. How can a man be so cynical?"

"That's not cynicism, Pashka. Someone who criticises a cannibal for not washing his hands before eating would be a cynic. There are simply no words to describe what that man did."

There is nothing special about cannibalism. People have been driven to it often enough, even in our century, during famines and the siege of Leningrad. But those were extreme situations. I'm curious to know how one human being could deliberately prepare another for the slaughter. I begin to chat to Cannibal after work, gradually broaching the subject that interests me.

Cannibal has spent most of his life in prison and is already in his sixth year at Ashkhabad. He doesn't look like a typical zek. He still has the physique of a sturdy peasant – which is what he was before he received his first sentence for stealing wheat. Physical strength enabled him to survive the camp mincing machine, but the experience taught him to believe in nothing but the principle, 'You die today and I tomorrow.' A morose man, Cannibal goes about his business in silence and never initiates a conversation. He subscribes to many papers and journals but it's useless to ask him to lend you something to read after work.

I never discover what I want to know. Cannibal tells me his only regret is ending up in jail; everything else he did was justified. To all my sly questioning he simply replies: "You'd have done the same in my place."

Cannibal has been behind barbed wire for so long he has forgotten what the outside world looks like. When a modern streamlined bus drives into the zone he breaks his usual silence: "Fuck me! Would you look at that – a train without rails!"

Like Cannibal, there are many zeks who have been in camps for so long they have grown used to their loss of freedom. They feel at home behind barbed wire. Several times I see a prisoner reach the end of his sentence only to be driven through the gates by force. One epileptic Kalmyk has no one waiting for him on the outside. He faces a choice between an asylum or life on a miserable pension. After his release he went into town and threw stones at shop windows until he was arrested and sent back to the camp.

The Uzbeks say that beautiful dreams are half our wealth. Poor is the man who has lost his dreams or has never had any in the first place; the camps are full of such people. Many Soviet citizens, especially peasants, live in such terrible conditions that they could swap places with a zek without noticing any difference in their standard of living. Both prisoners and free people eat the same disgusting food; the pitiful rags they wear are identical.

People on the other side of the fence often commit petty theft while shrugging off the consequences. 'They can't send me anywhere worse than prison; they can't give me less than a pound of bread,' goes the eternal refrain. When a person reaches that stage he is past caring what stupid crime he commits. Judges label as 'malicious' crimes that are committed out of simple despair, by people without beautiful dreams.

Every camp inmate develops a shell around himself but few are as hardened as Cannibal. At the other end of the scale are those who could discard their shells quite easily if only they were given the chance to live as a human being. One such zek is my friend Igor Alexandrovich. With his long thin head covered in prickly stubble, Igor looks like some kind of exotic cactus. We call Igor Alexandrovich by his full name and patronymic instead of the customary nickname. He earned this exaggerated respect by his singular behaviour. Years in prison have hardly affected his speech. He rarely swears and usually blushes when he does. He calls everyone by the formal 'you,' and speaks in the old-fashioned language of the pre-revolutionary intelligentsia. Igor Alexandrovich claims his father was an admiral who went over to the Bolsheviks after the revolution. Like all camp stories this is probably an exaggeration, but there is no doubt that Igor Alexandrovich comes from a refined background. What he knows about literature, music and theatre you don't pick up in camp libraries. He studied medicine in Leningrad but on graduating was arrested and sentenced to be shot under article 58. The sentence was later transmuted to ten years.

Igor Alexandrovich is ashamed of his record and will only say that he was imprisoned for practising illegal abortions. He has been in Kolyma and Norilsk. Because of his medical training he was put to work in camp hospitals. Thanks to that he survived.

Igor Alexandrovich was released after the 20th Party Congress but as a former zek his degree was no use. He went down to Central Asia where he found work in a Tashkent mortuary. After he lost his job through drinking he became a tramp and beggar.

Everyone likes to listen to Igor Alexandrovich's stories and it seems that he has come to believe his own inventions. He tells us he always carried at least two guns of foreign make, and that he has lost horses, women and dachas at cards. Famous actresses were in love with him and he hired whole restaurants for his week-long parties.

Because of his short sight, Igor Alexandrovich finds sewing difficult and so he never meets his work quota. This means he can't buy tobacco in the camp shop, and it leaves him squirming. Yet if I hold out my pack to him he declines with elaborate excuses. So I resort to a more devious method. Leaving a packet of *Prima* on my bench I go to the other end of the workshop. I return to find several crushed and broken cigarettes in my pack, where they have been too hastily replaced. From then on I resort to this method of giving Igor Alexandrovich a smoke.

Sometimes he's so overcome by shame that he drops his precious cigarette and has to scrabble around for it amid the grease and slime of the floor.

Igor Alexandrovich enjoys dispensing medical advice. When I cut my thumb he delivers a lengthy discourse on haemophilia. "On your release," he tells me, "you should go to take the waters at a spa. Preferably Karlsbad."

"I shall certainly follow your advice," I assure him.

A radio loudspeaker hangs over our heads in the workshop but it is hard to hear and anyway we aren't interested in the nonsense spewed out by Moscow. But when I catch the strains of an old romance, *Grief is my star*, I switch off my machine to listen. The noise of the workshop bothers me and I glance around in annoyance. No one else has stopped except Igor Alexandrovich who is standing with his head stretched up towards the loudspeaker. Tears as large as a child's roll down his stubbly cheeks. I don't know where he is at this moment but he sure as hell is not in prison. I turn away so that he won't notice me looking at him.

But later Igor Alexandrovich comes up to me. "Do you remember the song *Grief is my star*?"

"Of course, but I forgot the words."

"You don't need to remember them. Words only give a song its shape. When you love something or someone very much its form has no significance. All lovers know this."

Igor Alexandrovich is released several months before me and the camp is a sadder place without him.

Finally my own release comes. I intend to hang around in the town waiting for Death Number Two who gets out tomorrow. We plan to head for the Kuban where Death has some relations who might give us work. However the camp authorities have other ideas and they put me straight onto a train to Krasnovodsk, that most desolate of cities.

I have not been out of Ashkhabad for twenty-four hours before I'm robbed of my documents. In Krasnovodsk I meet an alkash with a cruel hangover and invite him for a drink. While we are seeing off our third half-litre he crowns me with a bottle. I wake up to find my pockets empty. At least I had the foresight to hide my money in a pouch under my collar. I'm not badly hurt but a few splinters of glass have embedded themselves in my scalp. 'Well, old son,' I tell myself, 'they say you're never too old to learn, but it seems you'll remain a fool till you die. Choose your drinking partners more wisely in future.'

I think it better not to hang around any longer waiting for Death. Without my release papers any cop could stop me and send me back to camp. Besides, I want to get out of Krasnovodsk. It is winter and the town is scoured by a cruel, sand-laden wind. I take a ferry to Baku and then a train to Tblisi.

***

According to legend, Bogdan Khmelnitski of Ukraine once summoned all the vagabonds in his kingdom to Kiev. He ordered straw of the best quality to be spread for them on the city's main square. When the tramps arrived they laid themselves down gratefully and went to sleep. Then Khmelnitski ordered the straw to be lit around the edges. As their bed blazed the tramps called out: "We're burning! Save us!" but none lifted a finger to help themselves. When the flames began to lick his feet their chief shouted: "How lazy you are, brothers! Why don't you cry out that I too am on fire?"

Soviet railway stations are like that square in Kiev. Their

warmth and 24-hour beer stands lure us vagrants like wasps to a jam jar, making it easy for the police to pick us up. We're aware of the danger but it makes no difference. In Tblisi I spend a few days hanging around the station, drinking in the buffet and trying to snatch a few hours' sleep in dark corners. Eventually my luck runs out. I am arrested and taken to the spets.

My cell is crammed with bare bunks. The small barred window lets in no sun so its light bulb burns around the clock. I've been drinking heavily for the past few days and fear the horrors will come on while I'm alone in the cell with no mental distractions.

"Hey, boss, give us a paper to read," I ask the sergeant when he brings my dinner. As I was being led to my cell earlier I noticed a pile of newspapers on a shelf in the corridor.

"They're old papers," says the sergeant.

"So what if they are. I'm bored to death," I insist.

"Do you really want something to read?"

"Well I'm not going anywhere in a hurry."

"Okay we'll give you a paper," there is a tinge of spite in his voice. An hour later the door opens and he throws in four newspapers. Eagerly I snatch them up and then drop them in disappointment. They are Georgian. I can make no sense of the tiny worm-like letters writhing over the pages.

As I pace around the cell I remember a Conan Doyle story called *The Little Dancing Men*, in which Sherlock Holmes deciphers a code made up of matchstick figures. Following his example, I resolve to make sense of those worms. However, unlike the great detective, I do not understand the language I am deciphering. The only Georgian word I know is 'beer.' Nevertheless, I remember that most surnames end in 'shvili,' so by looking for groups of five letters I'm able to work out the characters for sh, v, i and l. The paper's masthead 'Communist' is written in both Russian and Georgian, so that gives me 11 letters altogether. Pictures of Brezhnev and the cyclist Omar Pkhakadze add to my lexicon. Towards evening I am reading the paper aloud without understanding a single word. When the sergeant looks into my cell he can't believe his ears. He throws in a packet of *Prima*.

Reading helps pull me through my hangover. The guards tell me the odd word of Georgian which I have to memorise immediately as I'm not allowed pen or paper. Unfortunately my solitude soon ends. My cell fills with tramps and their endless discussions about where they have drunk and how much, what the women were like and who beat the shit out of whom.

While exercising in the yard, I see an old man sitting by the wall. He looks vaguely familiar. I go over and – oh Lord – it's Igor Alexandrovich. He has aged. Now he resembles a decrepit old lion whose shaggy black mane is grey at the roots where filth has not yet penetrated. Igor Alexandrovich screws up his eyes and studies me for a long time. Finally he mumbles: "Ivan Andreyevich! Is it you?"

"The very same."

"Have you been here for a long time?"

"I'll be out in a week."

"Which cell are you in?"

"Six."

"Would you be so kind as to take me in? Do you have enough room?"

"We'll make some."

Igor Alexandrovich jumps up and comes over to me. Bending his head close to mine he whispers: "Do you have lice in there?"

"Not until now," I reply, catching sight of a huge louse on his coat lapel. I point to it. Despite his poor sight, Igor Alexandrovich catches his household pet with a deft pinch and for some reason drops it into his pocket. Our exercise period ends and we are locked up again.

A tramp in my cell says that for the last few months he has seen Igor Alexandrovich begging in the subway near the *Collective Farmer* cinema. "When he has enough money he runs to the chemists for eau de Cologne, which he drinks from the bottle right there in the shop. When he gets too cold and tired in the subway he goes to the *Collective Farmer*. The cashier usually lets him in without paying. He sleeps through the double bill of Indian films, warms up a bit and then returns to his pitch in the subway. At night he dosses in a basement in Chelyuskintsev Street."

That evening the guards bring Igor Alexandrovich into our cell. They have sheared his mane and treated him to a half-hearted disinfection process. To keep him at a distance we put him to sleep on a separate bunk which we call the thieves' bed. Igor Alexandrovich takes this as a mark of special respect.

That evening he entertains us with a monologue on Rasputin. Our cell mates listen open-mouthed. Believing Rasputin to have been the lover of Catherine the Great, they hope to hear some dirty stories. Encouraged by his audience, Igor Alexandrovich strides up and down the cell, gesticulating wildly. Suddenly he stops in the middle of a word and crashes to the floor with an demonic cry. White foam bubbles from the corners of his mouth. We rush to help him, trying to make sure he doesn't bite his tongue. I have seen alcoholic epilepsy before in people who stop drinking too abruptly. We bang on the door, calling for a doctor, but the nurse has already gone home and the guards can't be bothered to ring for an ambulance.

Gradually Igor Alexandrovich's trembling ceases and he falls asleep, snoring loudly through his nose. We lift him onto his bed. We're all frightened. Perhaps every one of us is thinking to himself, 'That's my fate too.'

When Igor Alexandrovich awakens he remembers nothing. He rises and paces about the cell. We are all silent. He comes up to me, his head trembling: "Could you tell me the time please?"

"I left my watch at home on the piano."

"Yes, yes, it is easily done," he nods. "And may I ask what your name is, if that is not confidential?"

"Pushkin, Alexander Sergeyevich."

Igor Alexandrovich knocks at the cell door asking to be let out. When the sergeant comes he asks: "Would you be so kind as to tell me where I am?"

"Up your arse," replies the sergeant and goes off to lie down again.

After a few hours Igor Alexandrovich recovers his senses. I tell him about his fit. He sits on his bed lost in thought for a long time. Then he looks at me with tears in his eyes: "Finita la comedia."

As a doctor he understands very well what has happened and knows his end is near. "Ivan Andreyevich," he whispers to me, "I pray that death may come sooner rather than later. I would like to be done with this life."

The next day Igor Alexandrovich has another fit, an even more violent one. We make a terrible racket but still they refuse to call an ambulance. After all, it's not worth going to any trouble over an old beggar.

I do not see Igor Alexandrovich die for I'm released the following day and I take the first train out of Tblisi.

I go west, to the town of Zestafoni, joining a group of tramps who sleep under the carwash by the fruit market. Tramps regard Zestafoni as their capital, perhaps because the local police are lenient and no one has ever been jailed for vagrancy in this town. When the bazaar opens in the morning I earn a few roubles helping farmers carry goods to their stalls.

Most traders sell chacha under the counter. The police take their cut and turn a blind eye. Real chacha is made from grape skins but this is only for personal consumption. The bazaar variety is made from rotten fruit and anything that will ferment. Some brewers fortify their chacha with luminal and calcium carbide.

Near the entrance to the bazaar there are a couple of kiosks which sell odds and ends: envelopes, cosmetics and shoe-laces. They are owned by two Georgians, Archil and Soso. One evening as we sit outside the car-wash Archil comes up with a three-litre cask of chacha. He makes an offer: "I'll give you this if you pick up Soso's kiosk during the night and move it further away from the bazaar entrance."

"What about the cops?"

"I'll take care of them. You're not breaking into the kiosk."

"Okay."

We find an old telegraph pole, chop it into rollers, and at night move Soso's kiosk about 100 metres away from the entrance to the bazaar.

The next day Soso approaches us, offering another cask if we'll roll his kiosk back and drag Archil's away. This goes on for a week. There's no enmity between the two men; they're simply having a joke with each other. They have a sea of chacha and they think up this game out of boredom. Everyone has to find a way of entertaining himself.

There is a tramp in our circle who goes by the name of Lousy Vassya. Lousy Vassya has lived in Zestafoni for years. Everyone knows him; some even pity him. All year round he wraps himself in a dirty woollen coat which has not a single button. He likes to sit in the sun scratching himself. A tall and sturdy peasant, he's bloated from constant drunkenness and unable to do any form of work. From time to time a woman approaches Vassya and surreptitiously holds out a small medicine bottle. Reaching deep under his armpits he catches a few lice and offers them to the woman at a rouble a piece. His price is as stable as the London stock exchange. Georgian folk medicine recommends live lice as a cure for jaundice. They are stirred into yoghurt and fed unnoticed to the patient.

A few days before Mayday the bazaar director Vakho comes to us. "If you go on the First of May demonstration I'll give you a barrel of wine."

Tempted, we get down to business. We find a couple of poles and Vakho gives us three metres of red linen. We boil glue on our bonfire and mix it with chalk to make paint. Then we try to decide on a slogan. I propose *Lenin is with us!* but the others reject that as too inflammatory. *Peace to the World!* is too innocuous. Finally we agree on *Zestafoni tramps salute the First of May!*

Neatly stencilling the slogan, we hide the banner under the carwash and go around to other places in town where tramps congregate. Most of them sleep outside the metal plant where waste pig-iron is dumped. These tramps are distinguished by their burn scars and blackened clothing. Some agree to join us on the parade.

The parade begins with schoolchildren, followed by workers from the metal plant and then other factories and institutions. We infiltrate the contingent of shop workers, waiting till we are about 40 metres from the platform of dignitaries before falling into a group. This way the police have no time to seize us and pull us out.

The bigwigs on the platform know the order of the march so that they can shout appropriate slogans to each section.

"We greet the first of May with the highest respect for study!" they cry to the school children.

"Hoorah!" respond the kids with a half-hearted cheer.

"The world's youth are the vanguard of Communism!" they shout to the students.

"Hoorah!" cry the students, with even less enthusiasm.

"More goods! Cheaper and better!" they shout to the bazaar traders.

"Hoorah!" they mutter back, no doubt thinking, 'surely to God not, otherwise how are we going to survive?'

"A healthy mind in a healthy body!" they call to us, for according to their programme we should be doctors.

"Hoorah!" we roar at the top of our lungs, unfurling our banner. The loudest of all is Lousy Vassya. Pulling a hand out of his armpit he waves at the town's fathers. They stand in shock, rictus grins on their faces. As we march past I catch sight of them whispering to each other. I fear we won't see that barrel of wine, but I'm wrong. The barrel appears in the evening and we don't need telling what to do with it.

A few days later the police come to question us. Fortunately they only laugh and decide to overlook the matter. It would be too embarrassing to take us to court.

Not long after the parade Lousy Vassya overhears two Georgians arguing over whether anyone can drink a litre of chacha straight down. Vassya volunteers to try. He has been drunk since morning and wants to show off. He tips the bottle to his lips and swallows the chacha in great gulps. He just manages to draw the back of his hand across his mouth before he falls to the ground, black in the face. By the time someone has called an ambulance he is dead.

Vakho and many bazaar traders donate money to bury Vassya. We hold such a wake that it's a wonder no one follows Vassya to the next world.

11

Beggars

The 1980s

I grow bored of Zestafoni and decide to try my luck in the capital. Perhaps I'll cut down on my drinking, clean up and find some sort of permanent job.

On New Year's Day I arrive in Tblisi. This time I know better than to hang around the station so I take a trolleybus into town. Usually I avoid public transport: you can never get your bearings through the filthy windows. I prefer to walk the streets of a strange city to orientate myself. But this morning I'm tired and in urgent need of a hair-of-the-dog.

In the town centre I stop at a beer-stall. It's crowded and I have to look around for some elbow space. A voice growls: "Over here mate!"

I go across to three men, alkashi by the look of them. The one who hailed me sports a pair of broken glasses and a pointed beard. "Where are you from?" he asks.

"From where the wind blows."

"And where d'you stay?"

"Where the night finds me."

"And what do they call you?"

"Ivan."

"Ivan the what?"

"Just Ivan."

"Nothing in this world is simple. not even a boil can lance itself. I know Ivan Moneybags and Ivan the Terrible... Which one are you?"

"None. I'm from Chapaevsk."

"Let me see... the Terrible was the Fourth so that makes you Ivan the Fifth."

He holds out his hand: "Kalinin."

"Kalinin who?"

"Kalinin the Chairman of the Supreme Soviet!" he laughs. "Now we must drink to this meeting!"

Everyone rummages in their pockets. I offer a rouble but Kalinin puts out his hand to stop me.

"Today you're our guest!"

One of my new friends runs across the road to a wine shop and returns with a bottle of champagne. I'm disappointed, but Kalinin gives me a sly wink and approaches another table where several well-dressed Georgians are gathered. Wishing them a Happy New Year, he offers them the champagne. Then he returns to our table. In a few minutes the Georgians have sent over two bottles of champagne, a half-litre of vodka, and a dozen beers. We plunge into the beer and vodka. After a while we send the two bottles of champagne over to another group of Georgians. In an hour there are so many bottles on our table there's not even room to rest your elbow.

Kalinin used to be a physics teacher He really does look like the former Chairman of the Supreme Soviet of the USSR and he shrewdly exploits this resemblance.

"When I strike my pose on the Elbakidze bridge people stop and stare. Then they feel obliged to throw me a coin. You can find me on the bridge at any time; the cops leave me alone as long as I keep quiet. Trouble is, after I've had a few the urge comes over me to deliver a speech. My oratorical talent has landed me in the spets a few times."

When night falls Kalinin shows me a place to sleep. Under one of Tblisi's parks there is a cavern housing steam pipes that heat the city. In winter every railway prostitute, beggar, tramp and thief drifts to that cavern. Some are so weakened by illness and booze that they hardly ever leave the place. Others go about their business by day and gather again in the evening bringing food and drink. All night long the cavern rocks with songs, curses and fights.

It's a murky place, lit only by candles stolen by church beggars. Rats scurry over the bodies of sleeping tramps. The floor is covered in crusts of bread, slimy pieces of rotting liver sausage and shattered eau de Cologne bottles. Wine and vodka empties are collected early in the morning. We sleep on cardboard discarded by furniture stores. On my second night one of the sick vagrants dies. We all leave the cavern, someone tips off the police and we make ourselves scarce while they come to collect the body.

Hippies have made their appearance in Georgia by this time and some of them try to join us. We despise them as dilettantes and kick them out of the cavern whenever they hang around for too long. Once in a while, however, some Tblisi artist or intellectual decides he want to experience life in the lower depths – and offers to pay for the privilege. Then we put on a real feast with songs and folk dances. We tramps know perfectly well what's expected of us and earn the bottles that our visitors bring. Putting our arms around our free-spirited friends we spin endless yarns about our lives, sparing no harrowing detail.

One of our bacchanalia ends in a police raid. Nervous about entering our cavern, the cops send in dogs first. A tramp warns me that they'll use CS gas to flush us out if we don't leave of our own accord. As we emerge they throw us into waiting Black Marias. A cop grabs me but the confusion distracts him and I manage to slip away. I spend the rest of the night in the park and decide I will avoid the cavern in future.

The morning after the raid finds me wandering aimlessly down Plekhanov Avenue, hungry as a wolf-pack in winter. My head is a barrel of pain and grief; my brains splash about somewhere in its depths. I break into a cold sweat at the sudden hoot of a car. I feel that people on the other side of the street are watching me and whispering words of vicious condemnation. Penniless, I scour the beer-stalls but meet not a single acquaintance. I'm about to breathe my last yet I'm too scared to ask a stranger for a few kopecks. I slink along, keeping close to the wall and my eyes on the ground.

"Have you lost something?" says a voice above my head. A tall beggar stands with his back to the wall, propped up on two crutches.

"A purse - except I haven't lost mine; I'm hoping to find someone else's."

"No one's lost anything here today. That's for sure. I've been here since morning."

"Too bad," I say, moving off.

"Stop!" he cries, "Can you help me?"

"How?"

"I need to buy a bottle but I can't get to the shop."

"My pockets are empty."

"I've got the cash. I'll wait for you in that little square over there."

"Okay."

"My hangover's killing me," he sighs.

"Mine too."

He pours a pile of change into my hand.

"There's more than enough for a bottle here," I say.

"Buy two so you won't waste time running back to the shop later."

When I come out of the shop I see my saviour approaching the square, thrusting his crutches forward and dragging his paralysed body in their wake. I join him and we introduce ourselves. His name is Borya and he comes from Leningrad.

I discover that Borya is no drinker and only sent me for the wine because he guessed the state I was in. He drinks a glass to be sociable but refuses a refill.

"I've been paralysed since I was a student. I jumped from a train to avoid the ticket collector. If he'd reported me for travelling without a ticket the college would have cut off my grant. I had no family to support me. Since then I've been all over Russia. Once in a while the police pick me up and send me to an invalid home but I always run away. I arrive in some town or other and don't leave it until I've collected 1000 roubles."

"And then?" I ask.

"I bury them and go on to another town."

"Are you trying to save a lot of money – for retirement perhaps?"

"No. It isn't the money itself I need. I give away most of what I collect."

"But why d'you live like this? You stand the whole day long at your pitch, collecting money. You don't drink, you don't smoke and you give it all away?"

"The money is not the most important thing. I make people happy."

"How?"

"Imagine, I am standing on my pitch, virtually a corpse. A man goes by. I don't know anything about him. Perhaps he's a cruel person who beat his wife that morning. I've never seen him before and I'll probably never see him again. He notices me, fumbles in his pocket, finds a three-kopeck piece that's no use to him and chucks it into my cap. To me those three kopecks are nothing, but I've done something for that man."

"What have you done?"

"I've caused him to do good. When he passes on down the road he is a different person, although he may not know it himself. Even if he gave me the money automatically, without thinking, he's become a slightly better person."

I stare at Borya, as stunned as a bull in a slaughterhouse. He laughs. "I can see that you're not yourself yet. Here's some more money. I'm going to work. Meet me in Gorky Park this evening?"

"Agreed."

Borya pours some change into my hand, then he stands up. His body swaying like a pendulum, he returns to his pitch.

Anxious to continue our conversation, I do as Borya suggests and make for the park. As I near his pitch I cross to the other side of the street to pass unnoticed in the throng of pedestrians. The sight of me might remind Borya of his kindness; he's not in need of my gratitude.

Picking up a bottle of Imereti wine along the way, I choose a

far bench in the park where I can sit hidden behind some bushes. From time to time I take a slug of wine, trying to maintain myself on that blissful cusp between sobriety and drunkenness.

Long-suppressed thoughts churn in my mind: 'Who am I?' An alcoholic and a tramp. But I'm no white raven; half the country are alcoholics. Our alcoholics outnumber the populations of France and Spain combined. And that's only the men. If you count women too you have to add on all Scandinavia and throw in Monaco for good measure.

Unlike me, however, most people work, or at least give the impression that they're working. And for what? Just to drink away their pay at the end of the month. Many men claim they work for the sake of their family. But what's the good of an alcoholic in a family? How do they pay for their babies' milk? By collecting empty bottles? And I've seen children tremble at the sound of their fathers' footsteps. At least I had the honesty to ditch the pretence and take to the road, although it cost me my wife and daughter.

The worst thing you can do to someone else is humiliate them, but self-degradation is no less evil. The person who humiliates himself drags others down with him. I've seen this happen often enough and I don't want to be guilty of it too. Yes, I made the right decision back in that forest in the Kuban. I'm responsible only to myself now. Yet the one question remains: how am I going to live? I won't steal and it's hard to find work, so how will I buy my drink? In practice I'm almost a beggar, and I'm trying not to admit it. I shut my eyes to the truth. But when all is said and done I have to acknowledge what I am.

Why am I not ashamed to accept Borya's money while I refuse to hold out my own hand in the street? I don't consider myself better than him. It's not the first time a beggar has bought me a drink. I can't bring myself to beg, yet I drink at someone else's expense which is worse.

Another part of me interrupts: but beggars also live at others' expense.

No, I correct myself, beggars support themselves. They earn their kopecks through self-abasement.

All the same, I am mistrustful of beggars. I have known hundreds: on the streets, in camps, police cells and psychiatric institutions. Most of them are scoundrels and hypocrites. Many times I've heard them ask a passer-by: "Give me a few kopecks for the love of God."

When the person passes on they curse: "May you rot in hell you greedy bastard!"

I sometimes ask them: "How can you talk like that? It's up to them whether they give to you or not. Besides, people might overhear and what would they think of you then?"

"Fuck them. They are many and I'm only one. If one passes by another will drop something in my cap. Only God sees everything!"

But it's not for me to sit in judgment. Everyone lives as they can.

In former times whole villages worked as beggars, training their children to follow the family profession. These beggars roamed the countryside, pretending to have lost all their worldly goods in a fire. Others hung around stations asking for the price of a ticket, claiming all their money and documents had been stolen. In Astrakhan camp I met a man who spent years selling a saw outside Moscow stations. He worked with great artistry, dividing his time between Moscow's eleven termini. His victims were officers: none below the rank of major. He would go up to the officer, salute, stand to attention and bark: "Comrade Colonel! May I introduce myself? Sergeant-Major Sidorov, of the 187th Standard Bearers, guards division, Order of Suvorov!"

"What can I do for you, Sergeant-Major?"

"Excuse me, Comrade Colonel! Could you buy my saw?" Sidorov would bring out a wrapped-up saw from behind his back.

"But why should I buy your saw, Sergeant-Major?"

"I want to rejoin my family but I need 23 roubles for the ticket. I'll sell you the saw for five."

"Haven't you been to the Commandant's office?"

"Of course, Comrade Colonel, but as everyone knows, they're just a bunch of pen-pushers. They've never smelled gunpowder. I remember, now, near Breslau…"

At this point the colonel usually pulled out his wallet and gave Sidorov a 25-rouble bill. If the officer was at all suspicious he might ask: "Who was the commander at your Front?"

"Marshall Zhukov, Comrade Colonel!" replied Sidorov with shining eyes. "Now there was a true officer! He loved his men." Sidorov had learned the history of the 187th Standard Bearers off by heart. If the officer asked any tricky questions Sidorov would reply: "I don't remember. I was in hospital at the time, wounded in action."

Sidorov continued to offer his saw for six years. In the end people got to know him and he grew careless, accosting officers when he was already drunk. Finally he was arrested and sent to camp. But he was a born actor and the way I saw it he earned his drinks.

Like Sidorov and Kalinin, plenty of beggars earn their money through guile, but most play on pity. It is simpler and yields good results. I know that almost every human being is capable of feeling pity – perhaps even Cannibal – but I can't bring myself to exploit this feeling.

For my part, I admit I often earn my drinks through wit. I try to entertain, even when I don't feel like it. I survive by making people laugh. In a way my crippled leg helps because no one feels threatened by me.

Yet there is a difference between singing for your supper and holding out your hand for it. I fear begging as a way of life. It might be too easy. If I drop anchor outside some church or bazaar I might never return to a normal existence. And I still entertain hopes in that direction. Hope is the last to die and I clutch at it, sustained by memories of the past.

The evening is dark and rainy. When Borya arrives we take shelter in a half-constructed building near the park. I gather some rubbish and make a small bonfire. We spread newspapers on the cement floor and sit talking. I get completely pissed but Borya drinks nothing. He has a hot-water bottle tied to his thigh and urine trickles into it almost constantly. This embarrasses him so he tries not to drink, even refusing water.

Borya tells me more about his life. "Once I went to a public library in Leningrad to try to read something on begging, but I was disappointed. No one writes the truth. They slide over the surface of the question. Perhaps because they never write from the point of view of the beggar. Not even Dostoevsky. As for Tolstoy, he was a great sham. He went out punctually every day to give alms but before he would part with a kopeck he took away the beggar's very soul with his nosy questioning.

"The truth is, when I beg I inspire pity, and pity is always a blessing, no matter how dirty the soul in which it springs," Borya concludes.

"I can't agree with you," I say. "Pity is a good and natural emotion, but do you remember Yesenin's lines: *arousing tears in my heart is like throwing stones at the glass of my watch*? Only a wretch would deliberately try to awaken a person's compassion. It's a cheap thing to do."

Yet I can't criticise Borya for I realise that my way of life is essentially no different to his. The only distinction between us is that I don't see myself as a person who does good to others. Anyone who does good becomes a slightly better person himself, but if you plan in advance to do good then the deed loses all its grace. If I do good, then let it be by accident. Most likely I do no good at all in this world, and I certainly won't do so by begging.

Our divergent views spring from a more fundamental difference. "Borya," I observe, "you believe in God, but I don't. If there was a God there would be justice, and as there's none in this world, so there can be no God."

Borya objects: "But you can't judge God by your own standards of right and wrong. It is impossible to comprehend God. You simply have to believe."

"I can't 'simply believe' when life is so unfair. Why was I born here, now, in a country where it makes no difference which side of the barbed wire you are on? Why did you fall under a train?"

"Humanity doesn't yet have the wisdom to test whether there is justice or not,' Marcus Aurelius said that almost twenty centuries ago."

"Well that was 2,000 years ago."

"That only proves his point – the time has not yet come."

Borya and I arrange to meet the following evening but we miss each other and I never see him again.

***

I board the No. 5 tram on Klara Zetkin street. A man offers me his seat but I shake my head. When the tram moves I take off my beret and turn to the passengers.

> *Good health and good luck!*
> *Live as well as your pay permits,*
> *and if you can't survive on it,*
> *Well, then, don't. No one is forcing you!*

As I finish my verse the passengers burst out laughing. The words strike home, because no one can afford to live on their pay, not even the police. A woman holds out a 20 kopeck piece and asks: "You'll be getting yourself a beer with that, I suppose?"

"Not only beer but vodka too!"

She puts the coin back in her purse, finds a rouble and gives it to me. When I've worked the whole tram I get off, board the next one and repeat the performance. By the time I reach Collective Farm Square I have nearly 20 roubles. Some people grumble that I am just collecting money for my hair-of-the-dog, but I'm not offended. It's up to them whether they give or not. I'm not greedy. Having collected a little money I throw in the towel, buy a bottle and continue to drink throughout the day, inviting anyone who wishes to join me. I have no shortage of companions.

At night I open a bottle to see me through till morning. As I swallow my wine I am struck by guilt over the way I've earned it. The cycle of self-recrimination spins round my head as I try to fall asleep. 'What are you living for?' I wonder.

Next day I go to work on the tram again, and the next. Begging becomes a way of life that I no longer stop to consider. The police catch me a couple of times, but they either laugh at my verses or throw me off the tram.

Begging is not always as easy as it was that first day. Sometimes the trams are so packed I can't move among the passengers; sometimes they're too empty to be worth boarding. Then it rains for nearly three weeks. I freeze and fall ill. For a while I sleep at the top of a lift shaft in an eight-storey block of flats. I crawl up after midnight but I am eventually discovered by a resident who threatens to call the police.

My clothes are filthy and ragged, my shoes split, and I never have enough money for a new pair. I am desperately tired of spending the whole day on my feet. I long for a good night's sleep but the cops drive me out of the railway station and it's impossible to take a nap on the short Tblisi underground. Thank God for the bathhouse. It allows me to reheat my bones, but I can't linger for too long or they might throw me out and bar me from future visits.

Although I'm drinking a lot, alcohol is having less effect on me. Soon I need two or three bottles of fortified wine just to see me through the night, otherwise I can't even drop off for half an hour. When sleep comes it is crowded with nightmares.

There is a slope between the road and the river where townspeople tip their rubbish. In this place of unimaginable filth I can sometimes find unbroken bottles. The wine shop exchanges these for a bottle of Rkatseli.

At the top of the slope there is a small overhang. It gives me shelter and I'm unseen from the road. Here I huddle at night. The rubbish below me reeks of rotten meat and excrement, but the smell hardly bothers me. I lean back against the earth, with an open bottle between my legs, smoking and taking a swig of wine as soon as I start to feel bad. For months I have derived no pleasure at all from alcohol, but I need it to ward off the dt's.

When I've emptied my bottle I drag myself out of my lair and shuffle down to Klara Zetkin street. There, in a courtyard behind a little gate, is the 'fountain of life,' open 24 hours a day for the suffering and the greedy. When I open the gate the house-dogs barely stir; they must be used to night-time callers. I stumble through the courtyard and up a couple of steps to a veranda. Inside the veranda is a table with a three-litre jar of chacha on it. Beside it is a tumbler and a plate of bread and spring onion. An old woman sleeps on a huge bed beside the table – or at least she gives the impression of sleeping.

I lay my coins on the table. They are sweaty and crusted with tobacco. A withered hand shoots out from the bed, grabs the coins and stuffs them somewhere among a heap of rags. Having drunk my glass I slink out of the courtyard, shaking and trying not to throw up.

The devil only knows what those Georgians mix with their chacha. I break out in large boils like soft corns which itch and sting. I try not to squeeze them as I know that will make them worse, but when a boil the size of a walnut grows on my heel I have to burst it before I can get my shoe on. By the end of the day I can hardly walk for the pain. There are no bandages in the chemist. I go to Mikhailovski hospital but they throw me out because of my disgusting state. Finally the blood donor clinic where I occasionally earn a few roubles gives me a bandage. I rinse the wound under a tap in the street and bind up my foot.

After that I feel better and I'm able to do a little work on the No 5 tram. I'm not collecting much money these days, probably because I smell so bad that people turn their heads at my approach.

In the morning I grit my teeth and rip the bandage off my raw skin. I rinse it under a courtyard tap but can't wait for it to dry as I have to get to work. The damp bandage picks up dust and filth from the street. By dusk the wound is itching unbearably but I take that as a sign that it is healing. A few nights later I unwind the bandage to find a mass of worms writhing in the open flesh. I guess it will only be a matter of time before gangrene sets in. I fall into a stupor, staring at my foot as though it belongs to someone else.

That night on the rubbish dump I settle down with two bottles of Rkatseli to keep me going till dawn. I prop myself up against the bank, dropping off for a second, waking with a start and swallowing a couple of mouthfuls of wine. I keep a strict watch over the level of liquid in the bottle. Hold on, I tell myself, it's not evening yet! Reflecting on my situation I laugh out loud: "Look at you, my boy!" I even mumble a verse that comes into my head:

> *My room – a stinking garbage pit*
> *My bed – an old newspaper*
> *More than one tramp died here*
> *And so it seems, shall I*

I do not know whether I'll live till dawn, but I don't care too much either way. Let death come tonight. It'll put an end to life's torments once and for all. But I do fear the dt's. I fear I'll lose control and do something very bad. And I'm deeply ashamed of my filthy, festering body. I haven't been to the bathhouse for weeks; I can't use the communal pool because of my wound and I can't afford a private cabin. I'm filled with shame as I imagine the state my body will be in when it's found in the morning.

***

But I do not die on that Tblisi rubbish dump. In the morning I manage to drag myself out of my lair, gather some empties and limp over to the wine shop. I come out clutching a litre of fortified wine in each hand. As I cross Mardzhanishvili Square I trip and fall, instinctively flinging up my arms to save the bottles. My face slams into the asphalt, but by some miracle the bottles remain intact. With a groan of relief I pass out.

I awake to find myself lying on the pavement with a crowd gathered about me.

"We've called an ambulance," a voice says.

Thank God the police won't be involved, I relax and let myself be carried off to hospital. I don't care that my nose is broken and my eyes so swollen I can barely see; I fear only the dt's, which are fast approaching. Believing that I've witnessed a dreadful crime and the police want to interview me, I try to hide. I am also convinced that the perpetrator of the crime is tracking me down in order to kill me. In mortal terror of every living soul, I leap out of bed and run around the hospital, squeezing into dark cupboards and cowering under beds.

The staff finally catch me, put me in a strait-jacket and pack me off to 'Happy Village,' a large mental asylum in the mountains. There I'm cared for by an unusually kind young doctor who pays no attention to my repulsive appearance. She even suggests I go to a special clinic to have my nose repaired but I decline: "I'm not planning to become a film star; I need a psychiatrist not a surgeon."

The doctor orders me to be tied to a bed and then she injects me with Sulfazine.[36] With fiendish strength I tear off the sheets that bind me and run away. Although the staff have removed the handles of the ward doors I manage to prise them open with a dinner spoon. I run out of the hospital and down the road. Orderlies catch me two blocks from the clinic, drag me back and tie me up again. I get another shot of Sulfazine. My temperature soars. For two or three days I lie motionless, soaked in sweat. Gradually I return to my senses. When I admit to the doctor that no one wants to kill me she takes me off the Sulfazine and orders me to be untied.

Soon I am cracking jokes with the doctor and making her laugh. Through her contacts she finds me a job as a night watchman in a Tblisi theatre. With a roof over my head I'm able to keep off the drink for several months. One day, however, I run into Tolik, an old friend from Zestafoni who's trying his luck begging in the capital. He has nowhere to sleep. I can't recommend the cavern so we agree that after the theatre performance has ended Tolik will tap on my window and I'll let him in for the night. He sleeps curled up on some newspaper in a corner, refusing my offer of the couch: "No, no, Vanya, I piss myself after I've had a bottle or two."

Despite his alcoholism Tolik is so sharp he only has to look at a few lines of *Pravda* to arrive at conclusions we hear a month later on Voice of America. He tells me that something is changing in the USSR.

"But what difference will it make to our lives, Tolik?" I ask. "What happens in Moscow might as well take place on the moon."

---

36 A powerful tranquillizer.

The theatre management know about my weakness and try to keep me away from the bottle. However it seems churlish not to accompany Tolik when he pours his wine at night. Early in the morning he sneaks out, taking the empties with him. He spends the day begging and I give him some money from my pay to buy bottles for the night.

It's not long however, before we overdo it. The director arrives in the morning to find me sitting among the scenery as drunk as wine itself. Centre stage, Tolik strikes the pose of a Roman senator as he declaims Bezimensky's *Tragedian Night*. All around us roll empty bottles. We are puffing away like the *Battleship Potemkin*, although smoking is strictly forbidden in the theatre. They throw my friend out and call an ambulance for me. I am taken back to Happy Village and this time the doctor is not so kind.

***

I have been away from Chapaevsk for many years and hardly keep in touch with my family, apart from the occasional phone call to my sister. After my second cure I receive news from her that our mother has died. I go back to Chapaevsk for the last time, staying with my sister and her family. I don't understand them nor they me, but we are civil to each other.

My sister is the only family member I have left in Chapaevsk. Dobrinin died some years ago; Uncle Volodya moved to Ukraine. I hear he took to drink after he was widowed. My wife and daughter have been living in Estonia since they left me back in 1967. My sister occasionally gives me news of them.

I wonder whether to try to find out what happened to my real father. Since the time of Khrushchev I have accepted that he was shot. In the new climate of political openness it might be possible to learn details of his arrest and trial. But I decide it's better not to know the truth. If he was a Chekist he was probably responsible for sending people to their deaths.

My sister tells me there is some furniture left from our parents' house that she wants to sell.

"Keep the money," I tell her, "all I want is enough for a ticket out of this hell-hole."

"Where are you going?"

"Who knows? Fiji maybe."

And I really am thinking how good it will be to leave the country. Preferably forever.

Just before I leave Chapaevsk I run into a couple of old drinking acquaintances who are wending an unsteady way back from the cemetery. "Poor old thing," they say, after exchanging greetings with me: "They let us join the wake so it'd look as though she had someone to mourn her. We only knew her by sight; she died in the old people's home."

"Who was it?"

"Marusya Timofeyevna. Perhaps you knew her. She used to live in Bersol."

The dead woman was our old home-help, Cyclops. I pity her now, for her life turned out to be even more wretched than mine. After she left my parents she looked after children in other Party families until she became too old and infirm. She never married. The war left millions of surplus women and Marusya was last in the queue. Having no one to care for her, she entered the old people's home. It is the oldest building in town and worse than any strict-regime prison. The staff steal all the food and leave the inmates to decay in their own filth. As you pass the home you can see the old people standing outside on metal balconies, gazing forlornly at a world they have already left.

And that is where I'll end up if I stay in Chapaevsk, providing I don't drink myself to death first.

12

London

The 1990s

I have no reason to stay in Chapaevsk so I return to Georgia. The theatre takes me back as a watchman and I manage to stay sober for a while.

Change is in the air. Georgia no longer wants to be part of the Soviet Union. Civil war looms. My friends at the theatre fix me up with Georgian papers and take me with them on tour to the UK. I claim political asylum. I'll start life afresh.

At first I'm excited by my new surroundings. Like every naive Russian visitor I marvel at the shops. 'You could cover our walls with their toilet paper,' I write to my sister. It doesn't take me long to discover that vodka is cheaper than eau de Cologne. There's no need to drink substitutes when you can afford the real thing.

I discover too, that our propagandists didn't lie about the decadence of the West. People go around in clothes that would shame a Zestafoni tramp – and not only the poor: one day I see a young man walk out of an expensive restaurant in a *bushlat* – a padded grey Soviet prison jacket.

It shocks me to see a teenage girl put a bottle of beer to her lips. Back home even tramps rarely stoop that low; we keep personal drinking vessels. In any Russian park, if you look carefully, you'll see a glass under a hedge or bush, covered over with twigs to protect it from dirt. But perhaps we're more concerned with practicalities than appearances, for when your hands are shaking like death it is impossible to lift a bottle to your mouth. Besides, to spill a glass is a misfortune; to spill a bottle a tragedy.

But I soon get tired of the emptiness of the West. Here, people turn their lives into a ceaseless scramble for money. Most are rich beyond the dreams of a Chapaevsk citizen yet they are never content with what they have. Their system is a treadmill, not freedom.

All the same, I settle into life here, with my own room and a small pension. My furniture comes from the streets: chairs, mattress, sofa, vacuum cleaner, TV and a video that I repaired myself. At night I like to wander around my neighbourhood, seeing what I can pick up. Looking through people's rubbish, I learn a lot about them – what they read and what they eat, whether they're drinkers and whether they're ashamed of what they drink.

From time to time new arrivals from Russia come to stay with me while they get settled. They remind me of myself when I left home all those years ago. These young people expect the streets to be paved with gold, but they can only find illegal work as washers-up or cab-drivers. Some give up and go home again, tired of being treated as less than human.

I have begun a new career as an actor; some film students invited me to work with them. And I went to a studio and had my voice recorded for the new James Bond film *The World Is Not Enough*. They wanted a Russian speaker to curse like a sailor. I let rip, but in the end they only allowed me to use the mildest words.

Outside of work I hardly mix with local people. At my age it's

hard to learn a new language. Even if I could communicate we wouldn't understand each other. I'm not lonely; on the contrary, I sometimes long to go away from this city to a quiet village by the seashore, where I know no one at all.

Mostly I occupy myself by thinking about my past, trying to make sense of it. Like the disgraced teachers and engineers of Toliatti's market-place I always held the Soviet system responsible for my downfall. Throughout my life I felt plagued and persecuted by Komsomolists, bosses, judges and camp Godfathers. This isn't to say that when I poured myself a glass of wine in the morning I did it as an act of protest against the system. Of course not. But it consoled me to think that if I drank too much it was because I had no choice.

Now this old line of defence has fallen away. I am free from Komsomolists and Godfathers but I still drink. At least I know that whatever I have done, however deeply I have degraded myself, I shall pay for it. The thought cheers me slightly.

Despite everything I sometimes thank God that I became an alcoholic and took to the road instead of spinning out my days in Chapaevsk, talking of nothing but work and how many potatoes my allotment has yielded. I've broken through walls that confine the normal human being. I've discovered that things I once feared hold no terrors at all. Prison doesn't worry me; I can live by begging. I can live without a home, possessions or human companionship.

I've learned too, that there is no limit to how far a man can fall. Every so often you reach a barrier. No, you say, you have some pride left, you won't quaff furniture polish or drink in the street; you'll never hold out your hand and ask for money. But you do. People are like electric currents: they follow the path of least resistance, and it's easier to move downwards. The most terrible thing of all is that you get used to your degradation. Human beings can adapt to anything. And if ever a shadow of guilt or self-disgust darkens your door – alcohol soon chases off such unwelcome guests.

So I've discovered that my early fears were not so terrifying after all. Yes, I'm dependent on vodka, but that renders me independent of my surroundings, albeit temporarily.

Do I miss Russia? Perhaps not, yet still images haunt me of my past, particularly those days in the forest looking after the beekeepers' hives. I even feel nostalgic for the patter of raindrops on my tent roof and the sharp scent of herbs hanging up to dry.

But I haven't severed all my ties with the past; I even receive occasional letters from Olga. She never remarried. When my sister told her I had emigrated she started to entertain hopes, perhaps thinking I'd come off the bottle at last. Well I soon dashed those expectations; I told her that the West has given me no reason to stop drinking. Then she wrote back: *Come home Vanya, let us show you how to live.*

Her arrogance makes me angry. After all these years she still can't understand what led me to drink in the first place. I was not interested in becoming the ideal Soviet family man. The truth is, I just wasn't ready for a family at all. Yet at the same time her letter arouses feelings of guilt, especially towards my daughter, who is now ill.

Damn them all. I push the letter aside. What did they expect? At least I can be proud that I resisted their pressure to change into someone I am not.

I have to get out of the house. I pick up my stick and set off down the Romford Road. It is a typical English June day, blustery, the sky weighted with grey clouds. It starts to rain. Women huddle under bus shelters, adjusting their hijabs.

My sore kidneys twinge and the filthy air makes me wheeze more than usual. In the far distance seagulls wheel over the Barking dump, reminding me of my far-off days on *The Wave*.

As I pass a kebab shop I catch the eye of an acquaintance through the window. He rushes to the door:

"Vanya! Where are you going?"

"Hello Grisha. For a walk."

He falls in beside me. Grisha arrived a couple of years ago with his family. He usually takes great care of his appearance but this morning he is unshaven and his clothes are crumpled.

"I've left home. To teach them a lesson. My wife and her mother ganged up on me again. All I wanted was a Mercedes, for God's sake. I'm a man, aren't I? I can get credit but they said we couldn't afford it. I know my mother-in-law wants to humiliate me. She doesn't respect me."

Neither do I. But I like Grisha's mother-in-law and by giving Grisha a place to stay for a while I'll be lifting a burden from his family's shoulders. Besides, for once I feel like some company.

"Grisha, let things calm down. You can sleep on my sofa."

"Vanya, you've saved my life," he claps me on the shoulder.

We pass a supermarket. To cheer him up I suggest: "How about a bottle?"

***

The next few days are a blur. I wake up at the foot of my stairs with my pockets empty and my walking stick broken. My bones ache as though I've been beaten by a whole station of policemen. Grabbing the banisters, I haul myself up to my room. After swallowing the pain-killers my doctor gave me, I lie down.

The horror approaches. I stare into it like a rabbit transfixed before a cobra. I have to act while I can still think.

I call a friend, a young girl from Rostov. "Irina, I'm going to die tonight for sure. Call a taxi and take me to hospital."

"Ivan Andreyevich, you know the hospital won't admit you again."

"Excuse me for troubling you."

I put the phone down just in time. The mouthpiece has started to crackle with sounds I identify as Voice of America.

Irina is right. Since being in this country I've dried out in hospital four times. The detox clinic won't take me again either. Not that they're much use. They insisted on talking about my past, how I related to my father and other nonsense. They expected me to bare my soul to some young whelp with no knowledge of life. I begged them to give me injections, to knock me out while I got over the worst of the dt's. Surely the West must have discovered a cure for alcoholism; it is impossible they don't have that drug in their arsenal. But they refused me. They probably thought I was a drug addict to boot. So I drank all the mouthwash I'd brought with me and that wasn't enough. I managed to get to a phone and call Grisha, who brought in a hot-water bottle full of vodka. Somehow the doctors found out I'd had a drink and ordered me to leave. I lost my temper and raged at them but they would not relent.

***

Hours pass and with every minute I feel more scared. If only I can ride this one out I'll stop drinking for a while and then keep things under control like I managed to in Georgia. The TV flickers. Silent cues shoot coloured balls across the screen. They are not enough to distract me. Rain patters on my window. The street lamp outside my room casts a yellow pool onto the wet pavement. Tiny devils frolic in the gutter. If I drop my guard they'll climb up the drainpipe and slip in under the window frame.

I close my eyes and wait for night. Alarms wail in the distance. Cement mixers roar up and down the road. A sharp pain jabs through my leg; I sit up in time to see a devil running across the floor, squealing and brandishing his fork. I yell and Grisha hurries out of the kitchen with a bottle in his hand. Cradling my head in his arm, he wedges a pen between my teeth, unscrews the bottle cap and puts the neck to my lips.

Ivan's funeral is held at a North London crematorium. His friends want a Russian Orthodox priest to officiate, but none can be found. In the end a Greek priest comes from Kentish Town. Sunlight streams through the windows, illuminating the blue and gold of the priest's robes. Incense burns. We hold candles while St John of Damascus is read. In turn we step up to speak. One woman, Elena, can hardly force words out through her tears: "Why did such a lovely, generous man have to suffer so cruelly?"

When Father Constantine hears Ivan's story he returns his fee.

***

Forty days after Ivan's death Elena invites me to his *pominki* – his wake – in a flat on the North Peckham Estate.

I take the bus from Elephant and Castle to Camberwell Green, and then walk through back streets, past posters of the missing and the wanted.

Elena lives in a low-rise seventies building. She buzzes me in through metal security gates at ground level and again on her walkway. My path is blocked by a track-suited woman leaning over the railing: "They throw their chicken bones over the balcony," she yells at someone on the ground: "I've told the council but they do

fuck all. They want evidence. I'll show them fucking evidence…"
I squeeze past her backside to reach Elena's door.

She leads me into a room full of books and plants. A table is piled with salads in cut glass bowls. Solemn guests are seated around it. I recognise them from the funeral –Tatiana, Irina, Slava, Andrei, Vadim – young Russians whom Ivan did his best to help.

A teenage boy lumbers in. Elena introduces him as her son. He sports a black eye. He says he got beaten up at school for being Russian. "And they murdered a black kid, Damilola Taylor."

"Yes, I heard."

"Everyone knows who did it; the police know, but they haven't got evidence. The killers walk around like kings."

I wonder if this place is really worth leaving Russia for.

Ivan's photo sits on the mantelpiece. I recognise it as one I took on the day we visited his beloved *Cutty Sark* together. The finest ship ever built, he said.

"He was extraordinarily handsome as a young man," sighs Elena, "he showed me a photo once."

"I keep thinking I see Ivan in the street, out of the corner of my eye," says Irina.

"It happens to me too," I say. I catch myself peering hopefully at short, grey-haired men with walking sticks.

"He was so kind," Elena wipes away a tear, "like a grandfather to my boy."

"To Ivan," Slava proposes. We raise our glasses.

Mine contains water. Alcohol no longer has the desired effect and I know it never will again.

Slava sits opposite me. I marvel as he drinks his wine then refills his glass with orange juice.

A debate starts over Ivan's ashes. The women say they should go to his sister in Chapaevsk so that they can be placed beside those of his parents and brother; the men say he would have wanted them scattered over the sea. The women win.

***

"Are you going back to North London?" asks Vadim, a serious young man in glasses and a grey suit who works in software design. "I'll walk with you to the bus."

It is dark now and I am glad to have a companion. We set off through the estate to Camberwell Road. On the way Vadim explains that he comes from Moscow. He is in the UK on a work visa. He lives in the London suburbs – zone six. A world away from Ivan.

"Do you know that during one of his drinking bouts Ivan decided he was betraying his Motherland by claiming asylum here? He asked the Home Office to return his documents."

"Oh God, he didn't? I never heard about that."

"It was probably before you met him. When he sobered up he went down to Croydon. Andrei accompanied him – he was doing his legal training then. They explained that Ivan was drunk and didn't know what he was saying. They accepted his reapplication."

We step off the pavement as a group of hooded youths surge past.

"I doubt he'd have got away with it these days," I say.

"He got away with a lot in his life."

"How do you think he would have fared if he'd stayed in Russia?"

"I don't think he would have lasted so long – it's much tougher these days."

"I must say I'm amazed how understanding the Soviet system was of its drunks – holding their jobs open and trying to offer treatment. And Georgia was virtually a tramp's paradise…"

"Yes, but today's Russia is not a kind place for people like Ivan. If you don't shape up you're fired. There's no room for the vulnerable. I hate to think what could have happened to him if he'd stayed, he might have been murdered on the streets…"

We reach the bus stop.

"Are you going to the Elephant?" asks Vadim

"Yes."

"I'll come up with you, take the tube from there."

He flashes a sudden, shy smile. "Ivan told me about you. At first I was surprised that he was telling his story to an English person, but he said you'd lived out there."

"I did. I knew where he came from…"

The number 68 lurches towards us. We board and head off northwards.

ACKNOWLEDGEMENTS

I would like to thank Ben Yarde-Buller, my agent Peter Buckman, G.K. Darby, Conn McAfee, Paul Daly, Amy Spurling and Andrei Walton for their appreciation of Ivan's story; also Lana Feldman for introducing me to the brilliant Natalia Vetrova. Above all, I am grateful to Ivan for telling his story to me.